er earthy fresh non-toxic et

agrant living edible local herbal tasty

rt free-range colorful tender robust

natural juicy green ripe wholesome

nutritional accessible pure raw healthy

olesome tender earthy fresh non-toxic

isp robust fragrant living edible local

fibrous tart free-range colorful raw

local herbal tasty natural juicy green

-toxic leafy sweet nutritional accessible

agrant living edible local herbal tasty

natural juicy green ripe wholesome te

nutritional colorful tender crisp robust

accessible pure raw healthy fibrous

fragrant living edible local herbal ta

tender earthy fresh non-toxic leafy sw

fibrous tart natural juicy green ripe

leafy sweet nutritional colorful tender

herbal tasty accessible pure raw heal

tender crisp robust fragrant living edi

ripe wholesome tender earthy fresh n

pure raw healthy fibrous tart robust

Deliciously Organic

Deliciously Organic

CARRIE VITT

Photography by Helene Dujardin

INTERNATIONAL
FOCUS PRESS

Published by
International Focus Press
P.O. Box 831587, Richardson, Texas 75083-1587
www.ifpinc.com

For quantity purchases, please visit
International Focus Press online
or write to the address provided above.

ISBN 978-0963910387
Library of Congress Control Number: 2010928935
1. Cooking 2. Organic 3. Recipes

This publication contains the opinions and ideas of its author. It is intended to provide helpful and informative material on the subjects addressed in the publication. It is sold with the understanding that the author and publisher are not engaged in rendering medical, health, psychological, or any other kind of personal professional services in the book. If the reader requires personal medical, health or other assistance or advice, a competent professional should be consulted.

The author and publisher specifically disclaim all responsibility for any liability, loss, or risk, personal or otherwise, that is incurred as a consequence, directly or indirectly, of the use and application of any of the contents of this book. Before starting on a weight-loss plan, or beginning or modifying an exercise program check with your physician to make sure that the changes are right for you.

Printed in China
First Printing October 2010

To my husband, Pete

Thank you for your unwavering love and encouragement.
This book never would have come to be without you.

Contents

Thank You

My name may be on the cover, but an extraordinary team put this book together who never compromised the quality of their contributions.

First, though, I want to thank the Lord for putting health problems in my path, which led me to organic cooking. Nothing happens by chance, and I'm thankful for the opportunity to share what I've learned to help others.

Like most first-time authors, this book started at home. Pete, your love and encouragement drove me forward even before I knew I was to write a book. Hannah and Abby, you were my little sidekicks, ever giggling with love and excitement as you helped test Mommy's recipes. Mom, what can I say? Beginning when I was little girl, you lovingly taught me your culinary craft. For this book, you showed me the standard for testing recipes and so much more. Dad, thanks for teaching me to take risks and think on my own with clarity and vision.

My vision for this book was that the recipes would make the readers want to dive in. I thank the ever-talented Helene Dujardin, with her master's palate of food photography, for portraying how delicious organic dishes can be. What a joy to collaborate with you—even more precious that I gained a dear friend in the process. Helene also reaches millions through her blog "Tartelette."

For my cover shot and the one to the left, thank you, David Edmonson. You're not only one of the world's most celebrated photographers, you're truly selfless and ever-mirthful. For the wonderful family personality shots, thank you Luke Korem and Phillip Glickman. (Luke, I know you're my brother with a kick-tail production company, Sixth Seal Productions, but your photos rock!)

Thank you Jen Maki for really caring about getting the design right. (Did you ever think as childhood friends we'd one day work together like this?)

Then, there's the huge editorial team, many of whom are accomplished authors themselves. First, there's Paula LaRocque, IFP's editor-in-chief

and the author of numerous books (can't wait to read your first mystery novel, *Chalk Line*). Thanks for helping a first-timer cross the finish line. It felt as if you took my words, sprinkled fairy dust over them, and they came alive. Her husband Paul, the former ace editor for the *Fort Worth Star Telegram,* did the final sweep. Thank you Dianne Jacob, author of *Will Write for Food*, who meticulously edited the recipes, ensuring that all was in order. And, thank you Kim Pierce, for your invaluable editorial insight and contribution. Kim is also an author and for years was the heart of the *Dallas Morning News* food section.

Testing recipes is a daunting task. Leading the team was Cathrine Hughes who did all the metric conversions. Thank you for your friendship, encouragement, and painstaking effort. For the core of the testing, thank you Festive Kitchen icons, Jodi and Chrisie. You protected the integrity of my vision.

Thank you, dear Karin, for your help and constant encouragement and wisdom. Thank you also to the Breidenthal family: Brent, Brayden, Kyle, and Delayne—not only for being willing guinea pigs but also for honest feedback.

My publisher, International Focus Press, never compromised quality at any point—only asking what will make my book better as they directed the team. What a joy working with you. Your team was fantastic. When IFP passed the baton to Thomas Hummell at Toppan Press, he made sure a wonderful book was rendered. Thanks, Tom.

Thanks to the Waldrep and Wade families for opening their beautiful homes for the photo shoots. Thank you Kim Schuette, for providing me with the knowledge to stay healthy and giving me sound advice and help when I needed it most.

Finally, thank you to each and every one of my blog readers. Your constant support and comments keep me going. It is a joy to continue to create new recipes for you to use in your home.

CHAPTER ONE

Why I Made the Change

Why I Made the Change

If you had two girls, under the age of two, and your husband, a fighter pilot, was flying cover during a war in Iraq, would you be thinking about converting your diet to organic, whole foods? I wasn't. My life had enough stress without another distraction. But, that's what happened in 2003.

Two years earlier, after the birth of my second daughter, I began having daily migraines. I was 25. As migraines often are, they were both baffling and debilitating. They started with the birth of my first daughter, but were infrequent and not as severe. Now Pete was in harm's way in a dangerous place. The migraines increased to five or more a week. I often had to lie down in a quiet dark room, which was almost impossible with toddlers to care for.

I was taking several medications to manage the pain just to get through the day. They continued, though, four or more a week. After two years of struggle, my neurologist suggested adding yet another daily medication to my prescription regimen—a treatment that wasn't working anyway. I kindly rejected her suggestion and drove home thinking: *There must be another way.*

It's reasonable to surmise that the migraines increased in frequency and intensity because of the ever-present concern for Pete's safety and for those with whom he served, but I didn't think that was it.

The same day I saw my neurologist, a tiny newsletter article caught my eye while going through the mail. It was about the benefits of organic foods. I knew migraines could be related to diet, so I wondered if changing to organic foods might help. I was at the end of my rope and willing to try something different.

Relief

At the time, I was eating lots of vegetables to lose the last 10 pounds of baby weight. It's what mothers do, and I've always exercised and main- tained a healthy diet. It's how I was raised growing up in a suburb of Dallas. My mom, who was born in Louisiana, often served us Southern vegetable dinners. We rarely ate "junk" food. But I didn't know anything about organic foods, so I called a friend, Karin, to help me.

At the time we were based in Tucson. Karin's husband was also a pilot—and pilot's wives are usually very close. When we'd get together, the subject of food often came up. I noticed that her fridge was stocked up with organic ingredients and not packaged food. She told me they didn't use processed white sugar or white flour and everything was organic. I loved my friend and I thought that was weird, but I decided it was worth a shot. After all, I'd never yet heard of any- one developing disease or other health problems because they weren't getting enough pesticides, chemicals, preservatives, fillers, or other non-nutritive pseudo-food.

After reading the literature she gave me, I re- placed my lettuce with organic. It was my first step. I picked lettuce because it was the food I ate the most of. All my lettuce from that point forward was organic. It didn't matter if it was romaine, leaf, or butter.

Within a week I noticed a significant differ- ence. The frequency of my migraines decreased, and it was now easier to care of my kids. I didn't need any more encouragement. I next switched all produce to organic with the intent of increas- ing the amount of pure and untreated food in my diet and decreasing my pesticide intake. As I dug deeper and learned more, I continued making changes to my pantry and refrigerator. Over the next year and a half, I converted my family's diet to whole, unprocessed, organic ingredients.

Today, I have a migraine maybe once a month. I no longer need those expensive, powerful pre- scription medicines that only partially controlled the migraines. (I'm still waiting for a thank-you note from my health insurance provider—as I said, those pills weren't cheap!)

Although I experienced significant results, I

still had a measure of skepticism, which I probably picked up from my dad, an investigative journalist and author.

I'm Not Going to the Mountain!

Something that I didn't tell you is that Karin also grinds her own grain. When I started all this, Karin had two boys and was nine months pregnant with her third. One day, we were visiting and talking about organic food. When it was time for me to go, Karin, holding a big bowl of grain in her arms, said, "We have to go too because we're going to the mountains to grind our grain." I thought she meant the nearby mountains...and believe me, I thought that was way over the edge. I could only imagine Karin, hiking up the mountain trail with her two little sons in tow, finding the perfect rock on which to grind grain. Implanted in my mind was the outrageous image of my big-bellied friend grinding away on a rock overlooking giant gorges surrounded by Saguaro cacti. But, I didn't say anything. I just carefully thought about everything she suggested before acting.

Hilariously, I figured out later that what Karin actually said was that she was going to the Montains, friends of hers down the road! They had the grain mill, Karin didn't. When we got that sorted out, she said, "You must have thought I was a complete nut job!"

Not Yet Delicious . . .

As I began using organic, unprocessed ingredients, I felt like a stranger in a strange land. I had a hard time finding recipes that were equivalent in flavor to what we were accustomed to. Nevertheless, I avoided such ingredients as white sugar, white flour, and partially hydrogenated anything. Recipes using whole grains were especially challenging. We weren't ready to leave the world of paninis, pasta, and pizza, but just substituting ingredients didn't exactly work out. As my husband likes to say, we ate some terrible pancakes during the transition. This was disheartening because I had grown up with a great love for cooking that I inherited from the women of my family.

Rich Family Heritage

I'm blessed and grateful to be part of a line of wonderful cooks going back generations in Louisiana. They were foodies before the word "foodie" was invented. I come from a food-loving family of cooks, bakers, recipe creators, tweakers—and eaters. It was also common for the women in my family to parlay their love of cooking into both creative and money-making enterprises.

My great-grandmother, Ellis Hawsey, was an incredible cook who taught herself how to bake pies that she sold at a Baton Rouge country club to bring in extra money during the Depression. Because she was blessed to live 100 years, I had the privilege of spending time with her when I was a child.

Her gas stove fascinated me. I'd never seen another stove like it, with those blue flames that for so many decades had bought forth wonderful treats. To this day, when I smell the gas from a lit stove I think of her. I was also enamored by her large curio cabinet filled with teacups that sat in the corner of her living room. I stared at those teacups for hours. When I was ten, she let me pick out a few cups and saucers to keep. I chose three demitasse cups, never dreaming that one day I would have two daughters and that the three of us would use those precious cups during our occasional afternoon teas.

My Grandma Brice is the daughter of my great-grandmother. A remarkable Cajun cook and the wife of a Baptist minister, she's had the opportunity to cook for hundreds (maybe thousands) of church functions. When we visited my grandparents during my childhood, loads of gumbo, étouffée, and other Cajun treats awaited our arrival. Although they led a modest lifestyle, Grandma's cupboards and pantry overflowed with enough food to feed the entire family for a month! She even compiled two cookbooks with church parishioners—books that are still among my main resources. Whenever I need some good Southern ideas, I turn to the "yellow" and "green" books, as we call them. Grandma's cookbooks are a family treasure and some of the last few pristine copies were recently passed to my brothers' wives as wedding gifts.

When I was six, my parents sent me on a plane to visit Grandma and Grandpa. When I got home, they asked about my favorite part of my trip, and I proudly said, "Grandma taught me how to make biscuits!"

While I was researching and writing this book, I sat down with Grandma and we went through all of her recipes, handwritten on little note cards. A few are in this book.

And finally there's Mom, Grandma's daughter. She is an amazingly creative cook, teacher, and one of the top caterers in the country. I watched her build her company, The Festive Kitchen, which also has gourmet-to-go shops that regularly get top reviews.

When I was a little girl, Mom was very patient with me in the kitchen. She taught me everything from how to boil eggs to how to "whip up" Chicken Kiev. As a kid, I noticed that Mom read cookbooks as if they were novels—and then experimented. One Thanksgiving, for example, I remember her poring over her new Martha Stewart cookbook—then we made a turkey wrapped in puff pastry with pastry leaves and vines as a garnish. Mom was fearless in the kitchen.

After years of experimenting at home, Mom started selling Grandma's legendary fudge cake to the top hamburger joint in Dallas. I helped her make pans and pans of those cakes in our tiny kitchen, loading them in the back of our Cutlass Supreme (without air conditioning during the sweltering Texas summers, mind you) and delivering them every few days to the restaurant. Then a family friend, Catherine Liu, who owned a phenomenal Chinese restaurant, had Mom bake miniature cheese cakes for the first trade junket from China. Mrs. Liu, an author and a leading expert on Chinese cooking, told Mom she should start a catering company.

My mother was a trained labor and delivery nurse and full-time mother who didn't exactly have catering on her mind. She rejected the notion but kept baking cakes. Shortly afterwards, when I was twelve, a woman called and said she'd "heard" about my mother's catering company and wanted to book an event for a hundred guests. Mom's non-existent "company" obviously didn't have anything else booked, so she agreed. This, her first catering event, presented her with a steep learning curve as well as plenty of stress—to say the least—and she cooked way too much food. But her new venture, "The Festive Kitchen," was born.

The Festive Kitchen continued to grow and I grew with it, starting in the kitchen, baking and cooking, and later as a teen progressing to the wait staff. As Mom grew a multi-million-dollar business from the ground up, I worked everything from small luncheons to large, lavish, tented weddings. Today, my mother's company includes catering, retail stores, and a dedicated and creative staff. It has won many awards—even a Presidential White House Food Service Medallion for a dinner for 500 for the President of the United States.

From this rich, generational heritage I discovered the bedrock value of simple, delicious recipes paired with creativity and boldness in presentation. There is no doubt in my mind that Mom's tenacity to create with integrity was that seed planted deep in me necessary to navigate this new world of "organic."

I also decided that if we were going to eat organic dishes they were going to have to taste every bit as delicious as the ones I used before.

Deliciously Organic

This book isn't about giving up good tasting food for tree bark, as some might assume.

I started out by converting family favorites to organic. Sometimes, though, that didn't work as I replaced ingredients and I'd have to create my own. Believe me, I had many failures, but I kept tweaking things until I learned which combinations created the best flavors. And along the way, I learned how to gain access to unprocessed ingredients as well as how a typical American household can both function and benefit from a diet free of chemical preservatives.

Over time, I shared with my friends and family how I overcame my health problems. And then I told others. Many were earnestly interested in learning more or in making changes to their own diets. I continued to tell my story, share my adapted recipes, and give encouragement.

Observing all this, my husband asked me to consider writing a cookbook, especially when folks we hosted for dinner left with a stack of my recipes that I printed. What I saw as simple sharing—from one cook to another—Pete saw as filling a need.

Finally, the light bulb snapped on. What I was learning and collecting was a cookbook to be shared with others where the recipes used pure, whole, organic ingredients. From that moment, I couldn't stay out of the kitchen.

With the encouragement of friends, I began teaching cooking classes out of my home. My kitchen was perfect for demonstrating techniques to six or eight people. I had a blast bringing together people who didn't know anything about organics and equipping them with new knowledge.

Within a year of teaching those classes, I was overwhelmed with requests for information and recipes. So I started a cooking blog, *Deliciously Organic*, as an interactive and efficient avenue to teach and dispense advice and recipes on a much wider scale.

Every Recipe Professionally Tested

Have you ever prepared a recipe that looked terrific in a photo in cookbook but never seemed to deliver? Even in a book by someone you trust? Sometimes it's just innocent errors or incomplete directions. To make sure that this doesn't happen to you, I had every recipe professionally tested. I felt this was absolutely important because if you and yours don't like the recipes, it might discourage you from making this important change to organic cooking.

The testers I used were the ace testers from the Festive Kitchen, Jodi and Chrisie. Their job is to ensure that every Festive Kitchen recipe is duplicated day after day. And they are tough. If there's an error, they'll find it. And they found them! Most importantly, they truly loved the recipes and are adding them to their own diets.

It's About Common Sense

You may be surprised that I've even included a chapter for desserts. Just like some of the other dishes in this book, if you want to occasionally indulge, you can, but now it will be organic. Just be sure to use common sense as you plan your meals and diet. I also discovered that recipes that have saturated fats are even more satisfying when the ingredients are organic *and our family usually eats less*. Again, moderation is the key.

Especially important—If you choose to buy directly from a farm, such as beef and dairy products, be certain that they follow the strictest health codes. Don't be overly trusting. Just because suppliers say they comply with local and federal codes doesn't mean that all do. Be wise, smart, and safe.

Easy-to-use Tools to Help You

As the world of cooking is changing, so too are the tools we can now use with our cookbooks. Here are some tools you will want to use to make sure your transition to organic delicious cooking is simple and uncomplicated.

The Live Addendum—My publisher, International Focus Press (IFP), provides a unique "Live Addendum" for this book. This cutting-edge feature is an invaluable resource that allows me to provide you up-to-date information, including:

- New variations on recipes, especially those from readers.
- A "Vendor Source List" of recommended vendors for the ingredients and food you buy—which will be updated regularly. It's exciting to watch as ingredients that used to be difficult to purchase are now readily accessible. Be sure to check this online source list often and share it with your friends as you learn together.
- Updates of sources. Because scientific studies are always evolving, the scientific sources for many of the concepts in this book are provided in the Live Addendum. This ensures that you will have the most current updates. In addition, the latest studies and recommended readings will also be provided.
- Correction of errors that inevitably creep into even the best of books.

You can quickly find the Live Addendum on the IFP website at www.ifpinc.com.

Apps for your phone—I am in the process of creating apps you can use to make shopping easy and takes the guesswork out of remembering what you need to get. One app will provide a shopping list of all the key ingredients that you will want to change in your pantry. Then, when you go to the store and replace another ingredient, you just check it off, and the app shows you which ones you have left to purchase. It's also free and can be shared with your friends and family. Check out the Live Addendum on the IFP website for availability.

On Your Way . . .

I'm thrilled you're reading this book and hope my recipes will find a home in your kitchen. I also hope you'll discover, as I have, that eating food direct from the source—our earth—uninterrupted by fewer chemicals and less processing is not only perfectly doable and beneficial but also perfectly delicious! Just think of this book in your hands as a stack of great recipes—from one cook to another. And don't be surprised when your friends and the whole family (including the kids) say, "I can't believe this is organic. It's delicious!"

CHAPTER TWO

Before You Begin

Before You Begin

Now that you know a little about me and why I made the change to organic cooking, let me show you the ingredients I most often use, where they come from, and their benefits. The ingredients I've selected are readily available in most stores.

This chapter will give you a quick overview of what organic, unprocessed ingredients mean without getting too technical. (The source notes for many of the concepts presented are found on the "Live Addendum" for this book, which is located on the IFP website. Also, new and important studies confirming the importance of organic, "whole foods" to improve health will be posted there as well.)

The Resources chapter at the end of the book provides the sources for many of the ingredients. Because my list of favorite sources continues to change as the organic industry grows, the "Vendor Source List" will be updated regularly on the Live Addendum. Be sure to use this resource and print out a copy to take along with you when shopping or to share with friends.

Natural Sugars

Raw Honey

Raw honey is a natural sweetener that does not cause a rapid rise or fall of blood sugar levels. It is best to buy raw honey because it contains beneficial enzymes that are lost during processing and filtering. Honey is best used in dishes that don't need to be heated.

Organic Whole Cane Sugar/Sucanat

Organic whole cane sugar is dehydrated cane sugar juice and contains many minerals. I like to refer to it as "sugar before it hits the factory." Whole cane sugar be used in place of sugar 1:1 when baking and cooking. The rich molasses flavors do well in cakes and cookies or any recipe that would be complemented with a bit of a molasses flavor.

Maple Syrup

Maple syrup is rich in trace minerals and is an excellent sweetener for baking or drizzling.

Molasses

Molasses is the by-product from the production of refined sugar. Molasses is a rich mineral- and nutrient-dense syrup that is slightly sweet and is best used in baked goods.

Stevia

Stevia is a sweet powder that comes directly from the stevia plant and has become quite

popular in the last few years. It is 300 times sweeter than sugar so you need only a small amount to sweeten foods. It dilutes well in liquids and is perfect to sweeten hot and cold beverages.

Cacao Powder

Chocolate comes from the cacao bean. The nutrient-dense beans are ground to a fine powder and are a wonderful replacement for cocoa powder.

Sweeteners to Avoid:

It is best to avoid refined and chemically made sweeteners. Shop wisely. Many of the "raw" sugars on the market are simply white sugar with a bit of molasses added back to give them a brown color. Just check the labels, as described at the end of this chapter.

And remember, you can overdo unprocessed sweeteners as easily as refined sugars. So it's always best to eat unrefined sweeteners in moderation.

Oils and Fats

Healthy fats in your diet are essential to healthy living. Healthy "unrefined" fats enhance our immune and endocrine systems, are needed for energy, and help play an important role in the health of our bones. Olive oil, for example, that is unrefined, uses olives that have been pressed to extract the oil, but the oil itself hasn't been filtered, heated, treated with chemicals, and so on. In other words, without getting too technical, it's in its pure state.

In a world where our attention is brought to the "latest studies" it is important to understand which oils are beneficial for the body and which ones to avoid. Overall, it is best to consume unrefined oils. Unfortunately, these are sometimes difficult to find, but I've tried to remove most of the legwork.

While there are many excellent unrefined oils to choose from, here's a list of the ones that I use and are easily found at your local grocery store.

Coconut Oil

Coconut oil has gotten a bad rap over the last twenty years because many studies published about coconut oil were done on *hydrogenated* coconut oil. We should as a matter of course avoid hydrogenated oils of any kind—so be sure to read the labels.

Virgin coconut oil, processed without chemicals or high heat, is rich in medium-chain fatty acids that are quickly absorbed into the body for energy. This naturally saturated, but not hydrogenated, fat is getting renewed attention among researchers as it becomes clear that saturated fats have many vital roles to play in our bodies.

When buying coconut oil, make sure you buy organic, unrefined, centrifuged oil. To receive the maximum benefits you really want to find the best oil possible. Coconut oil is extremely stable so it is great to use when higher heat is necessary. In a typical recipe, coconut oil can be used as a replacement for other oils 1:1. If you are sautéing, however, I have found that you need less coconut oil than you may initially think because it has little water content, so use it very sparingly.

Butter

The best organic butter is butter from pastured cows, unpasteurized, and preferably cultured. Bright yellow organic butter is a good indicator of butter made with milk from grass-fed cows. If you can't find raw butter in your area then try to use an organic, cultured product.

Olive Oil

Olive oil is a wonderfully nourishing oil and is most beneficial when used in its raw form or processed at medium to low heat. Olive oil has a medium smoke point (visually starts to smoke) and so it's best to cook with it at a medium heat or lower to prevent oxidation, which breaks down the nutrients.

When buying olive oil, look for oil that is extra virgin, cold-pressed, and unfiltered. This can be difficult because there are no regulations on labeling olive oil in the United States. So, for instance, an oil labeled "cold pressed" or "unrefined" may not actually be so.

The first thing to do when searching for a good olive oil is to find out where it comes from. Call the company, visit its website, and find out exactly how it makes its oil. When you buy it, the olive oil should have a golden color and be cloudy (because it's unfiltered), and come in a dark green bottle to slow oxidation. The oxidation process creates free-radicals which can damage the body's cells. I've tried to make this search easier by listing my favorite brands of oil in Chapter 11.

Red Palm Oil

Red palm oil is a beautifully rich red oil that contains oleic and linoleic acid. It's a highly stable oil that adds a rich flavor to recipes and is my favorite for popping popcorn.

Sesame Oil

This is a stable oil that is great for cooking at high heats. I also love to add flavor by drizzling it over stir-fry before serving.

Flaxseed Oil

Flaxseed oil is rich in omega-3s and should be kept refrigerated until consumed. Since any heat will oxidize this oil, it should not be used to cook with, but rather only added to salads, smoothies, and other cold foods. It is best to use this oil in small quantities because the body absorbs it slowly.

Oils to Avoid:

Many of the oils used in the modern American diet can be hazardous to our health. They are processed, cleaned with chemicals, and most of them come from genetically modified corn or soy. Most oils found on the grocery store aisles are heated to very high temperatures during processing; this heat oxidizes the oils. Oxidation also creates free radicals that can damage the cells of our bodies, so it is best to avoid them. The processing increases the shelf-life of the oils and removes most of the natural flavoring, making them more attractive for the industrial food industry, but less attractive to the consumer. Vegetable oils, like canola and corn oil, are usually made with genetically modified corn, canola, and soy. So, I suggest you limit the use of such oils and stick with unrefined oils.

After you have taken the time to buy a good quality oil be careful not to destroy its good properties while cooking. Remember which oils have high smoke points and which have low smoke points so you will know which oil to reach for while cooking.

Keep in mind that even though you're not going to use certain processed vegetable oils in your cooking, it's almost impossible to completely avoid them if you are using processed foods, as they are found in thousands of packaged products. Therefore, make sure to read the labels on packaged foods to know what kinds of oils were used and choose products that use the most healthy ingredients.

Whole Grains

Whole grains provide many important minerals, oils, and vitamins that are vital to keeping the body performing at its optimum level. Industrial flour has been stripped, bleached and heated to provide a long shelf-life product that is neither nourishing nor tasty. While white flour may taste OK when combined with other ingredients, it contains minimal nutrients to nourish the body.

The main reason I like to use freshly ground grains is that they contain an amazing lightness and sweet flavor because the germ oil in the grains are still intact and have not gone rancid due to oxidation. When whole grain flour is stored at room temperature for over 24 hours, it begins to oxidize.

Grinding flour may sound like a huge task, but it only involves buying grain whole and then letting the grain mill grinder do the work. A grain mill is very similar to a coffee grinder. When you want the freshest tasting coffee, you grind the beans right before making it; the same is true with wheat and other grains. My grain mill is just another appliance in my home like a food processor or my standing mixer. It's about the size of a large modern ice cream maker. The grain is poured in on top, the mill is turned on, and within minutes you have freshly ground flour. There are also companies that will mill the wheat for you, and you can either pick it up at the store or have it shipped to you. It is important to remember to keep the flour in the refrigerator to slow the oxidation process. It will keep for about four or five days.

I understand that you might not have access to a wheat grinder or might not want to buy one, so I tested the recipes in this book using store-bought whole wheat pastry flour and had great results. Pastry flour is soft wheat flour that has been milled. It is important to buy your flour at a store with a high turn-over and keep your whole wheat flour in the refrigerator because the longer it sits on the shelf, the more it oxidizes.

Whole Wheat Flour

I use this grain the most because it is perfect for all kinds of baking. There are two different types of wheat flour:

- **Whole Wheat Pastry Flour:** Otherwise known as soft wheat flour, is best for baking muffins, cakes, pies, and biscuits because it has a lower protein count, has a buttery flavor, and produces a tender crumb. I use soft wheat for all of my baking except when I am baking a hearty loaf of bread.

  It is important to remember that fresh ground wheat pastry flour will produce a different texture than white flour bought at the store. When substituting white flour with fresh whole wheat pastry flour I generally recommend using 1 ¼ cups whole wheat pastry flour to 1 cup white flour.

- **Hard Wheat Flour:** Hard wheat flour has a high protein count so it is best used for baking bread, especially sourdough breads, and any other baked item that needs more gluten and structure. When a bag is labeled "whole wheat flour," it is generally hard wheat, be it red or white wheat.

Kamut

Kamut is a wonderful variety of wheat that has some of the same textures as cornmeal. I like to add it to baked goods when I want a grainier texture or some crunch to the exterior. It's great in whole wheat breads and wonderful in pound cake.

Corn

I recommend using organic corn because most of the conventionally grown corn in America is genetically modified. I like to grind my corn very coarse when I use it for polenta, grits, cornbread, or as a coating for meats and vegetables.

Nuts

It is important to soak raw nuts before eating because they may contain enzyme inhibitors that make it difficult for our bodies to digest them. Soaking nuts overnight or for seven hours will neutralize the enzyme inhibitors and make them easier to digest. I make large batches of soaked and dehydrated nuts and keep them in bags for quick snacks.

Soaked Method

Many experts believe it is beneficial to soak grains overnight (12 to 24 hours) before using them because they contain a high amount of phytic acid that is difficult for the body to digest. If grain is soaked overnight in an acidic liquid (such as buttermilk, crème fraîche, lemon juice, homemade whey, yogurt, etc.), the process is said to break down the phytic acid so the body can digest the nutrients more easily. Soaking grains is very simple. It takes only a minute or two of preparation the night before. I offer alternatives for soaking grains in most recipes so that you have a choice. If you have a hard time digesting wheat and other grains, I encourage you to try this method—you may find it solves that problem.

Milk and Cheese

Now please don't gasp when you read this, but I believe it is far healthier to drink safely produced raw milk from pastured cows as opposed to pasteurized milk. It is unsettling what has been done to our milk supply during the last hundred-plus years. Pasteurization began in the late 1800s and was meant to be a temporary solution until the dairy farms could find a cleaner way to process their milk. As the demand for milk increased it was realized that pasteurized milk could be industrialized and thus the milk industry began.

Wherever you see cheese listed as a recipe ingredient in this book, use cheese that is made from raw milk if it's available.

Pasteurization

Pasteurization is a process of heating milk to kill bacteria. Unfortunately, this process also typically destroys friendly bacteria (probiotics) and vitamins—including vitamin A and more than thirty percent of the vitamin B complex. When probiotic bacteria are destroyed, the milk becomes more vulnerable to contamination. After pasteurization, vitamins that were destroyed are often replaced with synthetic vitamins. One-and two-percent milk sold in stores may contain non-fat dried milk added to it. Non-fat dried milk is oxidized and therefore may contain oxidized cholesterol, which studies suggest may promote heart disease.

Homogenization

Homogenization is a process that takes place after pasteurization. In one method, for example, milk is pushed through small tapered tubes under high pressure to break apart the fat molecules. This is why homogenized milk doesn't have to be shaken—the cream does not rise to the top. Unfortunately, the structure of the fat molecules actually changes during this process. Not only are the new fat molecules difficult to digest, but they have also been linked to heart disease.

On the other hand, unpasteurized milk from grass-fed cows is full of nutrients and probiotics like lactobacillus acidolphilus, B6, B12, vitamins A and D, calcium, and it is rich in CLAs (conjugated linoleic acid). In other words, unpasteurized milk promotes good bacteria, sound digestion, healthy fats, and a healthy cardiovascular system.

Trying Raw Milk

If you've never tried raw milk, I encourage you to give it a try. The first time I tried it was at the farmers market. I drank it with my nose plugged in fear that it would taste horrible. To my surprise, it was the sweetest and creamiest milk I'd ever tasted. Whenever we have friends over who have never had it, I usually give them a glass. Every single friend who has tried it has been delighted to find how creamy and sweet it is. When I first started serving my kids raw milk my daughter said, "Mom, I love all of the sugar that you have been putting into my milk!" Of course, *be absolutely certain* that any direct supplier you choose complies with *all* local, state, and federal health and production codes. If you choose not to use raw milk in these recipes, you can substitute commercial pasteurized whole milk.

Meats

Beef

It's best to buy meat from pasture-fed cows (sometimes called grass-fed). Pasture-raised cows produce meat rich in CLAs (conjugated linoleic acid), omega-3 fatty acids, and is free from hormones and antibiotics. The best way to find pasture-fed beef is at a local farm where you can visit and see exactly how they raise their cows. I usually buy my meat in bulk from the farm and store it in the freezer so that I only have to shop for meat twice a year. Like dairy products, *be absolutely certain* that any direct supplier you choose complies with *all* local, state, and federal health and production codes.

Industrial or conventionally raised cows are fed a diet of genetically modified corn and sometimes animal by-products. They are also administered hormones and antibiotics to help them grow faster and to prevent infections that arise from the animals living on a corn-fed diet. Beef from conventional or industrial raised cows contains high amounts of omega-6s which is different from the pasture-fed beef that is rich in CLAs and omega-3 fatty acids. Before the beef gets to grocery stores, it's often irradiated. This helps destroy any bacteria in the beef but it may also destroy nutrients. (More on irradiation at the end of the chapter.)

Chicken

Chickens are another meat that has become industrialized. Chickens are packed into large pens and given a diet of genetically modified corn, soy, and often animal by-products. Pastured chickens, not to be confused with pasteurized, are allowed to roam freely and eat the bugs and foliage on the ground. These "free range" chickens have an increased amount of omega-3s and vitamin A when compared to industrial-raised chicken.

Fish

Farm-raised fish is quickly industrializing the fish market. Fish raised on farms are often fed fish meal that is made of ingredients such as animal by-products and by-products from the milling and food processing industries and are sometimes given additives that color their flesh. When looking for a good fish to buy, look for fresh fish that has been caught in the wild and is free of preservatives.

Spices and Condiments

It is important to buy organic spices because they don't contain pesticides and are free from irradiation, which is explained in detail at the end of the chapter. Irradiation is performed on almost all non-organic spices to increase shelf-life.

Herbamare

This is one of my favorite all-purpose organic seasonings. I use Herbamare on all sorts of meats and vegetables. You can also make your own spice mixes by reading the ingredients on the jars of your favorite seasoning mixes and then combining your own organic spices.

Salt

Table salts sold in stores today are bleached and cleaned with chemicals to remove the minerals, iodized, and then anti-caking agents are added. In contrast, unrefined sea salt is in its natural form, contains over 80 minerals and elements and hasn't been chemically cleaned. When buying salt, look for a hand-harvested and naturally dried product. My favorite is Celtic Sea Salt™. I prefer to use the coarse sea salt for most cooking and baking and keep a bag of ground sea salt for certain recipes that require a finer grain of salt such as a custard or meringue.

Condiments

Go to your fridge right now, pull out five of your most-used condiments and/or salad dressings and read the labels. Do you see high fructose corn syrup, hydrogenated oils, and preservatives that you can't even pronounce? These are the things that are overlooked the most because we tend to think that if we don't use them very often, they probably don't make much of a difference. But it does make a difference for our health. If your kids eat ketchup often, I recommend you switch to a ketchup that isn't loaded with corn syrup. If you have a busy life, but like to eat lots of salads with pre-made dressing, then the next time you go to the store look specifically for a dressing that isn't full of preservatives, sodium, and is packaged in a dark glass bottle (which prevents oxidation of the oils). Or, even better, make your own!

Reading the Label

Whole Wheat

Just because a product is labeled "whole wheat" doesn't mean that it is a hundred percent whole wheat. Currently, the label "whole wheat" means that there is some whole wheat in the product. If you are looking for a product that is one hundred percent whole wheat then the label needs to specifically say "100% whole wheat."

Natural

Currently regulations regarding the word "natural" apply *only* to meat and poultry products. Natural means that the meat or poultry contains no artificial ingredients or added coloring and is only minimally processed. Other than meat and poultry there are no regulations on the word "natural" and most food producers add this word to their label merely to increase sales. If a label says "natural orange flavor" this doesn't mean that the flavoring was made from oranges. It only means that the flavoring wasn't made from something man-made and the flavoring may actually be made out of corn or soy. The label "natural" is virtually meaningless unless it is on meat or poultry products.

Organic

If a label says "organic" it doesn't necessarily mean all the ingredients are organic. The only way to buy a product that is one hundred percent organic is to find one that's clearly labeled "100% organic."

Certified Organic

Today, "Certified Organic" means the food was produced without synthetic fertilizers, pesticides, hormones, antibiotics, food additives, is not genetically modified, and has not been irradiated, which often destroys healthy nutrients. (This definition will of course change over the coming years.) Farmers and food producers are allowed to use fertilizers and pesticides from natural sources. Organic meat and poultry may be fed only organic feed (without any animal by-products) and are not allowed to be administered any type of hormone or antibiotic.

Free Range

This simply means the animals are allowed access to the outdoors for a specified period of time—in some cases only five minutes. An animal may choose to remain indoors, but they have the freedom to go outside and have access to the sunlight. If you are looking for animals that were truly raised outdoors then look for the label "pastured."

Pasture Fed

This means the animal was *raised* on a pasture rather than being fed grain in a feedlot. This label does not always mean the animal was raised without antibiotics.

100% Vegetarian Diet

This means the animal was given a purely vegetarian diet which usually consists of corn and/or soy. Please remember that if it doesn't say "100%" there is no guarantee the animals were fed a full vegetarian diet. The natural diet for chickens and turkeys, for example, includes insects, worms, etc.

Grain Fed

An animal was given grains as feed. This does not mean they were always fed grain as they could have been supplemented with animal by-products. (Keep in mind that cows and lambs are herbivores and naturally eat grasses and not dry grains or legumes.)

No Hormones Administered

This label means no hormones were given during the life of the animal. By law in America, poultry and hogs cannot receive hormones, so this label leads a consumer to believe the company has done something extra, when in reality, they aren't allowed to give hormones in the first place. Please remember that even though a product says "no hormones" this does not mean that they were given any type of special diet nor is it guaranteed they were raised free of antibiotics.

rBST-Free

Many dairy cows are injected with rBST, also known as rBGH (recombinant bovine growth hormone), a genetically engineered growth hormone used to artificially increase milk production. As noted by leading organizations, inlcuding the National Institutes of Health and the American Cancer Society, more study is needed to determine that it is completely safe for human consumption. If a label says "rBST-free" this means the cow was not injected with growth hormones. All organic milk is rBST-free.

Genetically Modified Foods

Genetically modified foods are derived from plants or animals with DNA modified through genetic engineering. Genetically modified (GM) foods are allowed in the United States in the following foods and feed supply: alfalfa, canola, chicory, corn, cotton, flax, papaya, potato, rice, soybean, squash, sugar beet, and tomatoes. I encourage you to look more deeply into the effects of these foods especially since there has been no long-term testing on their effect on human health. Unfortunately, in America, GM products aren't labeled, so the best way to avoid them is to buy certified organic foods.

Irradiation

Irradiation is a process through which ionizing radiation in the form of gamma rays, x-rays, or electrons generated from machines are used to kill bacteria in food. Irradiation is now used for most non-organic produce, meat, eggs, and spices. Irradiation, however, destroys many of the vitamins in foods and, according to The Center for Food Safety, also doubles the amount of trans-fat in beef, which increases the risk of coronary heart disease. This process began as a solution to unsanitary practices on industrial farms. Irradiation also dramatically increases the shelf life of products. In America, irradiated food is only labeled if it is "materially" changed. Some companies have proposed labeling irradiated foods as "pasteurized"— a completely different process, but a term that's easier for consumers to accept. If you wish to stay away from irradiated foods, it is best to buy organic.

Additives and Preservatives

Regarding any of the ingredients in this book, I only use those that do not have additives or preservatives, including artifical coloring additives.

Key Points to Remember When Purchasing Ingredients

When you go to the grocery store or purchase specific ingredients online, be sure ingredients are clearly labeled "certified organic," which means they have been produced without synthetic fertilizers, pesticides, hormones, antibiotics, or food additives, and have not been genetically modified or irradiated. Be sure to read labels carefully, as some products are labeled organic without being 100% organic (they may be 95% organic).

When purchasing meat or dairy products directly from a farmer, be sure they are in compliance with all local, state, and federal requlations.

As always, be sure to use common sense as you plan your meals and diet. Moderation is the key when eating dishes with fats or desserts.

CHAPTER THREE

Simple Steps to Make the Change

Simple Steps to Make the Change

How to make the change: I understand the task of changing your entire diet to organic can seem overwhelming, especially if you're just now being introduced to things like organic whole cane sugar and coconut oil. I assure you that you can do it. I was in the same position several years ago when I swore to a friend that I would never grind my own grain, so I've come a long way!

There is a simple and practical way to make the change. The first step is to go through your pantry and fridge and read every label and identify the foods that have processed ingredients in them (see list below) as well as preservatives and additives. This will begin to help you identify the foods that you will eventually eliminate. When you're ready to start the change, begin by making one change every week. Discard one item and replace it with one new organic/unprocessed item in your pantry. After six months you will be amazed at how much change has occurred, and in a year or so, your entire pantry and fridge will be completely transformed. This was the approach I took because at the time I had two little kids and trying to convert everything at once was too daunting.

Below are a few check lists to help you clean out your pantry and fridge and replace those foods with nourishing, whole, organic foods.

Important when reading recipe ingredients: When reading the required ingredients for a recipe, if it says "½ cup cilantro, chopped," this means a ½ cup of cilantro and *then* it is chopped. If the recipe requires "½ cup chopped cilantro," then it requires ½ cup of *pre-chopped* cilantro. This is obvious for expert foodies, but will help the novice get it right.

Ingredients/Foods to Remove:

- Trans fats
- Canola oil
- White flour
- White sugar
- Corn oil
- High fructose corn syrup
- Vegetable oil
- Sunflower oil
- Safflower oil
- Soybean oil
- Hydrogenated oils: oils labeled refined, hydrogenated, or partially-hydrogenated

Please remember that every food or item below and all ingredients used in this book are organic and unprocessed, even if not specifically noted. For ingredients you can make yourself, the page number for the recipe is provided.

Ingredients/Foods to Add:

Sweeteners:
- Whole cane sugar or Sucanat
- Raw honey
- Maple syrup
- Molasses
- Maple sugar

Oils and Butters:
- Extra-virgin, cold-pressed olive oil
- Centrifuged, extra-virgin coconut oil
- Raw, unsalted butter
- Red palm oil
- Sesame oil

In the Fridge:
- Pastured eggs
- Mild, raw Cheddar cheese
- Cultured cream cheese
- Pastured butter
- Raw milk and cream
- Mascarpone cheese
- Crème fraîche (p. 200) or a cultured sour cream
- Kombucha
- Ohsawa nama shoyu, fermented soy sauce
- Raw apple cider vinegar
- Raw sesame oil

For Baking:
- Whole wheat pastry flour
- Hard white wheat flour
- Raw cacao powder
- Vanilla (p. 212)
- Almond extract
- Aluminum-free baking powder
- Arrowroot powder

Other Items:
- Steel-cut oats
- Brown rice (p. 207)
- Brown rice pasta
- Whole wheat pasta (p. 198)
- Black beans
- Tea
- Dark chocolate

Seasonings:
- Herbamare is a fantastic seasoning mix to use on just about any savory dish
- Celtic Sea Salt (from the Grain and Salt society)
- All seasonings in my pantry are organic *and* non-irradiated.

Rise and Shine!

Healthy Tips to Start Your Day

- Start your day of with a tablespoon of coconut oil. Coconut oil will give you energy and a dose of healthy fat to start the day

- For a "fast-food" oatmeal breakfast option, soak your oats the night before.

- Buy eggs that are pastured and organic. Pastured and organic eggs contain high amounts of carotene, omega-3 fatty acids, and vitamins.

- Hard boil a few eggs and keep them in the refrigerator for a quick and nourishing breakfast.

- Keep freshly ground flours in the refrigerator so they stay fresh longer and are on hand for morning pancakes and muffins.

- Keep frozen berries on hand for a quick morning smoothie.

- If you sweeten your tea or coffee, start substituting honey for sugar. For the first week use half honey and half sugar and the next week use all honey. And, if you use cream, switch from your daily preservative laden creamer to organic cream or coconut milk.

CHAPTER FOUR

Breakfast and Brunch

✕

Breakfast and Brunch

Sour Cream and Lemon Pancakes with Blueberry Puree

I love making these pancakes in the summertime because of their fresh, clean flavor. The tart lemon pancake paired with the bright burst of sweet blueberries is one of my favorite ways to start the day. **MAKES 18 3-INCH (8 CM) PANCAKES, SERVES 4-6**

:::

1 ½ cups (240 gr) blueberries

6 tablespoons maple syrup

1 cup (240 ml) sour cream

2 large eggs, room temperature

2 cups (260 gr) whole wheat pastry flour, preferably freshly ground

2 teaspoons baking powder

1 teaspoon baking soda

1 teaspoon salt

6 tablespoons whole cane sugar or Sucanat (see p. 18)

¾ cup (180 ml) lemon juice

About 6 teaspoons coconut oil

:::

Puree blueberries and maple syrup in a food processor. Pour into a small saucepan and heat over low heat.

Whisk together the sour cream and eggs in a small bowl. Whisk together flour, baking powder, baking soda, salt, and whole cane sugar in a large bowl. Make a well in the center of the dry ingredients and pour in the sour cream mixture and the lemon juice. Quickly fold the ingredients together until just combined.

Heat a 12-inch (30 cm) skillet over medium-high heat for 3 minutes. Melt 1 teaspoon of coconut oil in pan and swirl to coat. Using a ladle, pour ¼ cup (60 ml) batter onto 3 spots on the skillet. Cook pancakes until large bubbles appear, about 1 minute. Using a thin spatula, flip the pancakes and cook until golden brown on second side. Remove pancakes from pan and top with warm blueberry puree. Repeat process with remaining batter and coconut oil until all pancakes are cooked.

VARIATION: See **Soaked Method** (p. 23). Whisk together flour and sour cream in a large bowl. Cover and leave at room temperature overnight. When you are ready to make the pancakes, add baking powder, baking soda and salt to soaked mixture and stir until fully combined. Whisk together eggs, lemon juice, and whole cane sugar in a medium bowl. Pour into flour batter and whisk until just combined. Let sit 5 minutes before cooking pancakes. Cook the pancakes according to the recipe above.

Pecan, Coconut and Cherry Granola

If you come to my house, you won't find a single box of cereal in the pantry because I make homemade granola served with milk. It's a hit with all ages and so much healthier. You can substitute just about any nut or dried fruit in this recipe.
MAKES ABOUT 8 CUPS (880 GR), SERVES 16

1 cup (185 gr) whole cane sugar or Sucanat (see p. 18)

¾ cup (180 ml) maple syrup

4 cups (440 gr) rolled oats

1 ½ cups (130 gr) coconut, unsweetened

1 ½ cups (150 gr) dehydrated pecan halves or pieces (see p. 213)

1 cup (160 gr) dried cherries, lightly chopped

Preheat oven to 350°F (180°C) and adjust oven rack to middle position.

Whisk whole cane sugar and maple syrup in a small saucepan over medium heat until almost smooth. Pour oats, coconut, and pecans into a large bowl and then pour the syrup on top. Stir until syrup coats the oats, coconut, and pecans. Spread out on a large baking sheet lined with unbleached parchment paper and bake for 20 minutes.

Cool completely, break into pieces, and then add dried cherries. The granola will keep for several weeks in an airtight container.

VARIATION: See **Soaked Method** (p. 23). Pour oats into a large bowl and cover with water. Add 1 tablespoon of lemon juice and stir. Cover bowl and leave at room temperature overnight (at least 8 hours). The next day, preheat oven to 150°F (70°C) and adjust rack to middle position. Drain the oats and press gently to release excess moisture. Pour oats onto a large baking sheet and spread into a thin layer. Dehydrate in oven overnight or until crispy. Add coconut and pecans, combine well, and pour sugar and syrup mixture on top. Stir until syrup coats the oats, coconut, and pecans. Bake at 150°F (70°C) for 4 hours until dried. Cool to room temperature and toss with dried cherries.

Tomato Basil Quiche

This is a scrumptious and simple-to-prepare quiche. It's best to use pastured eggs as they contain more carotenes, fat-soluble vitamins, and omega-3 fatty acids than conventional eggs. Pastured eggs can be found at your local farmers market, CSA (Community Supported Agriculture), or health food store. This quiche can be baked in either a pie dish or a 9-inch tart pan. **SERVES 8**

¼ cup (30 gr) shredded mozzarella

1 pie shell, baked and cooled (see p. 202); or baked and cooled in 9-inch tart pan as shown in photograph

3 cups (540 gr) ripe Roma tomatoes, thinly sliced (about 4 tomatoes)

¼ cup (60 ml) fresh basil leaves, slivered

2 tablespoons minced fresh chives

3 large eggs, beaten

⅓ cup (80 ml) raw heavy cream

⅓ cup (80 ml) whole milk

½ teaspoon Dijon mustard

¼ teaspoon sea salt

¼ teaspoon freshly ground black pepper

Preheat oven to 400°F (200°C) and adjust rack to middle position.

Sprinkle mozzarella over baked and cooled pie shell. Layer tomatoes, basil, and chives over the cheese.

Whisk eggs, cream, milk, mustard, sea salt and pepper in a medium bowl. Pour custard over chives and bake for 30–35 minutes, or until lightly golden brown.

Cheesy Egg and Mushroom Scramble

This recipe is a version of what my husband made for me when we were dating. I would come over to his place after work and he would scramble some eggs and mushrooms and serve them in warm corn tortillas. I think the combination will surprise you. **SERVES 4**

::

8 corn tortillas, preferably Ezekiel brand

7 large eggs

1 tablespoon heavy cream

3 tablespoons unsalted butter, plus more to butter your tortillas

4 ounces (115 gr) cremini mushrooms, cleaned and sliced

½ teaspoon garlic powder

1 cup (70 gr) grated Cheddar cheese

Sea salt

::

Preheat oven to 350°F (180°C). Place the corn tortillas in an ovenproof dish, cover, and heat until warm, about 10 minutes.

Gently whisk eggs and cream together in a large bowl.

Melt the butter in a 12-inch (30 cm) skillet over medium heat. Add mushrooms and sauté until they release their moisture, about 12 minutes. Make an opening in the center of the mushrooms and add the garlic powder. Stir the garlic in the middle of the pan until it becomes fragrant (about 30 seconds) and then stir into the mushrooms.

Pour the eggs into the pan and top with the cheese. Increase temperature to medium-high. Stir continuously with a large spatula until the eggs are cooked to your liking, about 1–2 minutes. Season with sea salt before serving.

To serve, butter a tortilla (and if you like, sprinkle a little sea salt on it) and top with the eggs. Roll it up and enjoy!

Gingerbread Pancakes

Nothing says "fall" to me like a plate of gingerbread pancakes smothered in butter and drizzled with maple syrup. The aroma of cinnamon, ginger, nutmeg, and cloves filling the kitchen will get even the sleepiest of kids out of bed. **SERVES 8-10**

3 large eggs, separated into a bowl of whites and a bowl of yolks

½ cup (70 gr) muscovado sugar

2 ¼ cups (530 ml) whole buttermilk (see p. 203)

½ cup (120 ml) whole milk

¼ cup (60 ml) brewed herbal coffee

10 tablespoons unsalted butter, melted, divided

3 cups (390 gr) whole wheat pastry flour, preferably freshly ground

1 ½ teaspoons baking powder

¾ teaspoon baking soda

¾ teaspoon sea salt

1 teaspoon ground cloves

1 tablespoon ground cinnamon

1 tablespoon ground ginger

1 tablespoon ground nutmeg

¾ cup (180 ml) maple syrup

Coconut oil or butter for frying

Whisk the egg whites and muscovado sugar in a large bowl until well combined. Add buttermilk, milk, and herbal coffee and stir to combine. Whisk 6 tablespoons of melted butter with egg yolks in a small bowl and add to the coffee custard. Stir until combined.

In another large bowl, whisk together the flour, baking powder, baking soda, salt, cloves, cinnamon, ginger, and nutmeg. Add liquid ingredients to the dry ingredients and quickly whisk together until just combined. Let sit for about 5 minutes before cooking.

Heat remaining 4 tablespoons butter and maple syrup in a small saucepan over low heat. Heat a 12-inch (30 cm) skillet over medium-high heat for 3 minutes. Melt 1 teaspoon of coconut oil in pan and swirl to coat. Pour ¼ cup (60 ml) batter onto 3 spots on the skillet. Cook pancakes until large bubbles appear, about 1 minute. Using a thin spatula, flip the pancakes and cook until golden brown on second side.

Repeat process with remaining batter and coconut oil until all pancakes are cooked. Drizzle warm maple syrup and butter over pancakes and serve immediately.

If you want to make some of these ahead of time, fry pancakes as noted above. Place them on a cooling rack set over a cookie sheet, and slide into the oven heated to 170°F (80°C) to keep them warm. The cooling rack will keep the pancakes from getting soggy.

VARIATION: See **Soaked Method** (p. 23). The night before, stir together flour and buttermilk in a large bowl. Cover tightly and leave at room temperature overnight. The following day, stir in the baking powder, baking soda, salt, cloves, cinnamon, ginger, and nutmeg. Whisk the egg whites and muscovado in a large mixing bowl. Melt 6 tablespoons butter and whisk together with egg yolks in a small bowl, then add it to the egg whites and sugar.

Add the wet ingredients to the flour batter. Stir until well combined. Let sit for 5 minutes before proceeding with recipe.

Banana Bread Bruschetta

Here's a quick, simple brunch recipe that turns ordinary banana bread it into something unexpected. The toasted bread is smothered with creamy ricotta cheese and topped with bright apricot preserves so you get toasty, crunchy, creamy, and fruity all in one bite. **SERVES 8**

8 thin slices of banana zucchini bread (see p. 53)

1 cup (240 ml) ricotta cheese

¼ cup (60 ml) apricot preserves

Preheat oven to 350°F (180°C). Place banana bread slices on baking sheet in one layer and bake for 12 minutes or until toasted. Remove from oven and cool to room temperature.

When ready to serve, spread 2 tablespoons ricotta cheese on each piece of bread. Add a dollop of preserves on top. Serve immediately.

Strawberries and Sweet Cream

This simple fruit dish goes well with any brunch or breakfast. The crème fraîche is smooth and silky against the sweet, plump strawberries. It's best to buy whole flaxseeds and grind them just before using to receive the optimum nutritional benefits. **SERVES 4**

::

1 cup (240 ml) crème fraîche (see p. 200)

¼ cup (60 ml) maple syrup

2 pints (580 gr) strawberries, hulled and sliced

Ground flaxseeds

::

Whisk together crème fraîche and maple syrup, cover, and let sit one hour in the refrigerator to allow flavors to meld. Serve over strawberries and sprinkle with flaxseeds.

Baby Butterball Chive Biscuits

These are the perfect biscuits to serve at brunch. They're little balls of buttery-flakiness that are completely addicting. I always make double the recipe because they disappear quickly. **MAKES 18 BISCUITS, SERVES 6-8**

2 ¼ cups (340 gr) whole wheat flour, preferably freshly ground

2 teaspoons baking powder

2 teaspoons coarse sea salt

1 cup (225 gr) unsalted butter, cold, cut into tablespoons

1 cup (240 ml) sour cream

⅓ cup (15 gr) chives, minced

Preheat oven to 375°F (190°C) and adjust oven rack to middle position.

In the bowl of a food processor, pulse together flour, baking powder, and salt to combine, about two 1-second pulses. Add butter and pulse for ten 1-second pulses. Pour the dough into a large bowl and add sour cream and chives. With the back of a spatula, firmly fold the dough until it comes together and is slightly tacky.

Place dough on a floured surface and roll out until ¾-inch (19 mm) thick. Use a small 2-inch (5 cm) biscuit cutter to cut biscuits. Place each biscuit on a cookie sheet lined with unbleached parchment paper. Bake for 20 minutes or until golden brown.

If you don't want the mess of rolling out the dough on the counter, use a small 1-inch (2.5 cm) cookie scoop to scoop the dough right out of the bowl.

Oats with Maple Syrup and Cream

Oats with cream is a staple breakfast in our home. Since I soak oats overnight, the next morning I can have breakfast on the table in about five minutes, which is perfect on those busy mornings. On the weekends, or when guests come over, I like to spice it up a bit using pecans, walnuts, dried fruits, and cinnamon to make it a bit more special. **SERVES 4**

1 cup (200 gr) steel-cut oats
1 tablespoon whole buttermilk (see p. 203)
Maple syrup
Cream

The night before, soak your oats in a bowl with 1 cup (240 ml) of water and the buttermilk. Leave the bowl on the counter at room temperature.

The next morning, bring 1 cup (240 ml) of water to a boil in a medium saucepan. Stir in oats and turn heat down just a little to keep it from boiling over. Stir frequently until most of the water is evaporated and oats are thick and creamy.

Serve with a drizzle of cream and maple syrup.

 If you need extra energy in the morning you can also top your oats with a teaspoon or two of coconut oil.

Banana Zucchini Bread

As a kid, I remember Mom sneaking zucchini into her loaves of banana bread to get extra vegetables into our diets. It worked and I do the same for my kids. Now, my kids giggle when they tell their friends about the "hidden" zucchini. **MAKES ONE LOAF, SERVES 8-10**

:::

3 tablespoons unsalted butter

3 tablespoons coconut oil

2 ½ cups (325 gr) whole wheat pastry flour, preferably freshly ground

1 cup (185 gr) whole cane sugar or Sucanat (see p. 18)

½ teaspoon sea salt

1 teaspoon baking soda

3 very ripe bananas, mashed

½ cup (60 gr) grated zucchini

¼ cup (60 ml) buttermilk (see p. 203)

2 large eggs, room temperature

1 teaspoon vanilla extract (see below)

:::

Preheat oven to 350°F (180°C) and adjust rack to middle position. Butter a loaf pan.

Melt butter and coconut oil in a small saucepan. Cool slightly. Whisk flour, sugar, salt, and baking soda in a large mixing bowl. Stir together mashed bananas, zucchini, buttermilk, eggs, melted oils, and vanilla in a medium bowl. Pour wet ingredients into dry ingredients and gently stir until just blended.

Pour batter into the loaf pan and bake for 50–55 minutes or until golden brown and a toothpick pressed into the center comes out with a few moist crumbs attached. Cool for 10 minutes and then run a knife around the outside to loosen the edges. Turn loaf out onto a cooling rack and cool before serving.

You may choose to use homemade vanilla in place of vanilla extract. The recipe can be found on p. 212.

Raspberry Almond Muffins

I came up with these muffins one morning as a change from the usual blueberry, and they were a huge hit. I generally freeze a large batch so I can reheat them in the oven on rushed mornings. **MAKES 12 MUFFINS**

::

3 cups (400 gr) whole wheat pastry flour, preferably freshly ground

1 tablespoon baking powder

½ teaspoon baking soda

½ teaspoon sea salt

8 tablespoons unsalted butter, softened

2 tablespoons coconut oil

¾ cup (140 gr) whole cane sugar or Sucanat (see p. 18)

2 large eggs, room temperature

1 teaspoon vanilla extract (see p. 212)

1 teaspoon almond extract

1 ½ cups (350 ml) whole buttermilk (see p. 203)

1 ½ cups (190 gr) frozen, organic raspberries

::

Preheat oven to 375°F (190°C) and adjust rack to middle position. Whisk flour, baking powder, baking soda, and salt in a medium bowl and then set aside.

Cream butter, coconut oil, and whole cane sugar for 2 minutes on medium-high speed in the bowl of a standing mixer. Add eggs, one at a time, beating well after each addition. Add the extracts. On medium-low speed, beat in half of dry ingredients in two batches, alternating with the buttermilk until just combined. Remove bowl from mixer and gently fold in the berries. Using a 2-inch (5 cm) cookie scoop, spoon muffin batter into buttered muffin cups until ¾ full. Bake 25–30 minutes or until golden. Cool for 5 minutes before serving.

VARIATION: See **Soaked Method** (p. 23). Stir together flour and buttermilk in a large bowl. Cover and leave at room temperature overnight. The next day, add the baking powder, baking soda, and salt and whisk to combine. The dough will be very thick. Cream 1 cup whole cane sugar, butter, and coconut oil for 2 minutes on medium-high in a standing mixer. Add eggs one at a time, followed by both extracts. On low speed, add flour mixture in small pieces (I like to pull pieces off by hand, about 2 tablespoons each), one at a time and continue until all pieces are added. Turn off mixer and stir a few times with a wooden spoon to make sure all of the batter is blended. Fold in raspberries. Using a 2-inch (5 cm) cookie scoop, spoon muffin batter into buttered muffin cups until ¼ full. Bake for 25 minutes until golden. Cool for 5 minutes before serving.

Brie and Walnut Crisps

Thick, triple-cream Brie is like a pillow of buttery-goodness on the tongue. Put it in a cracker with butter and walnuts, bake it until crispy, and you have a wonderful addition to any brunch menu. They also make satisfying hors d'oeuvres or a summertime snack when paired with an ice cold glass of rosé. **MAKES 25 CRISPS**

::

4 ounces (115 gr) double or triple cream Brie, rind removed, room temperature

½ cup (115 gr) unsalted butter, room temperature

¾ cup (115 gr) whole-wheat flour, preferably freshly ground

⅓ cup (40 gr) chopped walnuts

¼ teaspoon sea salt

2 dashes cayenne pepper

Herbamare seasoning (see p. 25)

Paprika

::

Pulse together Brie and butter in food processor until smooth. Add flour, walnuts, salt, and cayenne and process until dough is smooth and just comes together in a ball. (Dough will be very soft.)

Place a sheet of parchment paper on the counter. Pour dough onto its surface and form into a log. Wrap the remaining parchment paper around dough and then roll dough on the counter until it stretches into a log about 2-inches (5.1 cm) thick. Refrigerate for 3 hours.

Preheat oven to 400°F (200°C) and adjust rack to middle position.

Unwrap dough and slice into ¼-inch (6 mm) thick slices. Place each round on a baking sheet lined with unbleached parchment paper.

Bake for 10–12 minutes or until edges are just golden brown. Remove from oven and sprinkle lightly with Herbamare and paprika. Cool before serving.

Strawberry Coconut Smoothie

This is a quick, heart-healthy and energy-providing breakfast for hectic mornings. The smoothie is creamy and sweet with little hearty flecks of flaxseeds. You can pour it into a travel mug and drink as you go. It's full of omega-3 fatty acids, lauric acid, and fat-soluble vitamins and will keep you going for hours. **SERVES 1**

¾ cup (180 ml) coconut milk

¼ cup (60 ml) water

1 tablespoon flaxseeds or hemp seeds

½ cup (100 gr) frozen strawberries

1 tablespoon coconut oil

1 raw large egg yolk

1 tablespoon raw honey

Place all ingredients in a blender and process until smooth. The flaxseeds or hemp seeds will be ground up when blended which will allow your body to use the nutrients in the seeds.

If you aren't comfortable using a raw egg yolk, you can omit it.

Hot Chocolate with Maple Marshmallows

This is a new twist on an old winter favorite that uses nutritious organic maple syrup instead of sugar and only takes minutes to prepare. A variety of flavorful syrups, including light and dark ambers, are available in many stores. For something extra special, top off the steaming mug with maple marshmallows. **SERVES 4**

::

4 cups (950 ml) whole raw milk

5 tablespoons maple syrup

5 tablespoons cacao powder

1 teaspoon vanilla

Dash of cinnamon

Maple marshmallows (see p. 193)

::

Whisk all ingredients except marshmallows together in a medium saucepan over medium heat. Continue to whisk to dissolve cacao into milk (this will take a minute or two). Warm until steaming, stirring frequently. Pour into mugs and serve, and for a unique variation, drop in a couple of maple marshmallows.

Buttermilk Coffee Cake

It took me years to come up with this buttery, sweet, whole-wheat coffee cake. When I was a teen at summer camp, the cooks whipped up batches of coffee cake on Sunday mornings. This recipe, using only the purest ingredients, is a close replica of the rich cake they served. Best eaten the day it's baked. **SERVES 6-8**

8 tablespoons unsalted butter, room temperature

1 ¼ cups (230 gr) whole cane sugar or Sucanat (see p. 18), divided

2 large eggs, room temperature

1 teaspoon vanilla extract

¾ cup (180 ml) sour cream

2 ¼ cups (300 gr) whole wheat pastry flour, preferably freshly ground

2 teaspoons baking powder

½ teaspoon baking soda

½ teaspoon sea salt

3 tablespoons unsalted butter, cold

1 tablespoon maple syrup

2 teaspoons ground cinnamon

½ cup (100 gr) whole walnuts or pecans

Preheat oven to 375°F (190°C) and adjust rack to medium position. Butter an 8 x 8-inch (20 x 20 cm) baking dish.

Cream 8 tablespoons butter and ¾ cup (140 gr) whole cane sugar in the bowl of a standing mixer for three minutes on medium-high. With mixer on low, add eggs and vanilla, blending well. Add sour cream and blend well. Remove bowl from mixer.

Whisk together flour, baking powder, baking soda, and salt in a small bowl. Add dry ingredients to the wet ingredients and stir with a wooden spoon until combined. Pour batter into the baking dish.

In the bowl of food processor, pulse together 3 tablespoons cold butter, remaining ½ (90 gr) cup whole cane sugar, maple syrup, and cinnamon. Pulse until combined, about 5–6 pulses. Add nuts and pulse about 6 times until nuts are roughly chopped. Crumble topping on top of batter. Bake for 25–30 minutes or until golden brown.

Pumpkin Muffins

On chilly fall days, I experiment with all kinds of pumpkin recipes. These light and fluffy whole-wheat muffins use coconut oil. To get as much coconut oil in my family's diet as possible, when baking, I substitute a couple tablespoons of the butter for coconut oil. **MAKES 16 MUFFINS**

::

4 tablespoons unsalted butter, softened

2 tablespoons, coconut oil

1 ⅓ cups (245 gr) whole cane sugar or Sucanat (see p. 18)

½ cup (120 ml) pureed pumpkin

2 large eggs, room temperature

½ teaspoon vanilla extract (see p. 212)

1 ¾ cups (230 gr) whole wheat pastry flour, preferably freshly ground

¼ teaspoon baking powder

1 teaspoon baking soda

1 teaspoon sea salt

½ teaspoon ground cinnamon

¼ teaspoon ground cloves

⅓ cup (80 ml) whole buttermilk (see p. 203)

½ cup (50 gr) chopped pecans (optional)

::

Preheat oven to 350°F (180°C) and adjust rack to middle position.

In mixer bowl, beat together butter, coconut oil, and sugar on medium-high speed for about 2 minutes. Turn mixer to low and add the pumpkin. Add eggs one at a time, blending well after each addition. Mix in vanilla.

Combine flour, baking powder, baking soda, salt, cinnamon, and cloves in a large bowl. With the mixer on low, add half of the dry ingredients, followed by half of the buttermilk. Repeat process and mix until just combined. Fold in pecans, if using. Spoon batter into oiled muffin tin cups until ¾ full. Bake for 23–25 minutes, or until golden brown. Cool for 5 minutes before serving.

Feeling Fresh

The Best of the Garden

- It's not hard to grow your own herbs. All you need is a few small pots, and a sunny window. Start with basil, thyme, oregano, and rosemary. It's a budget-saver, plus, it's fresher than herbs at the store.

- To determine if an avocado is ripe, gently press on the skin. If it leaves a small indentation, it's ready. To ripen, just leave the avocado out on the counter for a couple of days. Store in the refrigerator once it's ripe.

- Mix any of the salad dressings in this chapter and store in a glass jar. When you're in a rush, you'll have organic salad dressing available free of additives and preservatives.

- To retain their flavor, it's best to store potatoes, onions, garlic, and tomatoes at room temperature.

- The skins of vegetables and fruits contain fiber and vitamins, so keep the peels on!

- Buy a bag of lemons and squeeze a little juice in your ice water throughout the day. The lemon juice helps detoxify the liver.

- Eat beets—another detoxifier.

- Organic produce doesn't always look "perfect"—and that's okay!

CHAPTER FIVE

Salads

Salads

Roasted Red Onion and Pear Salad

I created this dish on a whim several years ago for a *Cooks Country* magazine contest. Six months later, after I'd completely forgotten about the recipe, I received a call saying I'd won the grand prize. I was so thrilled and tickled because I had lost the recipe! As soon as the magazine arrived, I invited friends over to try the prize-winning salad! **SERVES 4**

1 medium red onion, cut into 1-inch (2.5 cm) wedges

2 tablespoons coconut oil

2 tablespoons fresh squeezed orange juice

1 tablespoon fresh squeezed lemon juice

1 teaspoon Dijon mustard

1 teaspoon honey

½ teaspoon fresh thyme, chopped

¼ teaspoon sea salt

¼ teaspoon freshly ground black pepper

¼ cup (60 ml) extra-virgin olive oil

1 head Bibb or butter lettuce

8 cups (170 gr) baby spinach

1 ripe Bartlett pear, cut into bite-sized pieces

½ cup (55 gr) goat cheese, crumbled

¼ cup (25 gr) dried cranberries

Preheat oven to 400°F (200°C) and adjust oven rack to middle position.

Toss onion wedges with coconut oil. Transfer to baking sheet and roast until brown and soft, 25 minutes, flipping wedges halfway through cooking. Cool for 15 minutes.

Whisk orange and lemon juices, mustard, honey, thyme, salt, and pepper together in medium bowl. Gradually whisk in olive oil.

Divide Bibb lettuce leaves among individual salad plates. Toss spinach with ¼ cup (60 ml) dressing in large bowl. Divide spinach among plates. Arrange roasted onion, pear, goat cheese, and cranberries on top. Drizzle with remaining dressing and serve.

Cherry Tomato Caper Salad

This summer salad is quick to prepare after you've been out all day. It's tangy, refreshing, and will complement just about any dish. It is best served at room temperature the same day it is made. **SERVES 4**

::

¼ cup capers, drained

3 tablespoons balsamic vinegar

4 teaspoons extra-virgin olive oil

2 pints (950 ml) cherry tomatoes, halved

¼ teaspoon sea salt

⅛ teaspoon freshly ground black pepper

10 large fresh basil leaves, chopped

::

Combine the capers, balsamic vinegar, and olive oil in a small bowl and stir. Place the tomatoes in a medium bowl and drizzle with the dressing. Toss gently. Season with salt and pepper and let salad sit for 15 minutes to let flavors meld. Sprinkle with chopped basil and serve.

Thai Steak Salad

If I could only eat one salad for the rest of my life, this would be it. The heavenly combination of mango, mint, cilantro, and avocado amazes the taste buds. To save time, you can cook the meat and noodles ahead of time and store them in the refrigerator until you're ready to assemble the salad. **SERVES 4 AS A MAIN COURSE**

8 ounces (230 gr) buckwheat soba noodles

1 pound (450 gr) ½-inch thick good quality grass-fed sirloin steak, trimmed

Sea salt and freshly ground black pepper

1 tablespoon coconut oil

8 cups (170 gr) baby field greens

1 ripe mango, cut into 1-inch (2.5 cm) pieces

4 green onions, chopped

10 mint leaves, chopped

½ cup (120 ml) cilantro, chopped

2 avocados, cubed

1 teaspoon fish sauce

4 teaspoons organic whole cane sugar, or Sucanat (see p. 18)

4 teaspoons fresh squeezed lime juice

6 tablespoons extra-virgin olive oil

2 tablespoons sesame oil

2 tablespoons soy sauce

2 tablespoons fresh minced ginger

2 cloves garlic, minced

1 teaspoon sesame seeds

Fill a large pot with water and bring to a boil. Cook noodles according to package directions. Drain and rinse with cold water.

Season both sides of sirloin with salt and pepper. Heat a large skillet (not nonstick) over medium-high heat for 2–3 minutes. Add coconut oil and swirl to coat. Place steak in skillet and cook for 2 minutes without moving until well browned. Flip and cook another 2–3 minutes until the other side is browned. Transfer the meat to a large plate and loosely tent with foil. Let rest for 5 minutes.

Toss field greens, mango, green onions, mint, cilantro, avocado, and cooled soba noodles in a large bowl. Whisk together fish sauce, sugar, lime juice, olive oil, sesame oil, soy sauce, ginger, and garlic in a small bowl. Pour dressing over salad and toss well. Slice steak into thin ¼-inch (6 mm) strips, against the grain at a sharp 45 degree angle. Sirloin has distinct lines (striations) in it. If you cut with the grain, the meat won't be as tender.

To serve, divide salad onto four plates and top with slices of sirloin. Sprinkle with sesame seeds. Serve immediately.

White Corn Salad

This is a simple side dish I've made for years when the weather is stifling hot. The cold sweet corn, ripe tomatoes, and green onion are like a cool splash of summer. I usually pair this with my quesadillas and some fresh margaritas. **SERVES 4-6**

2 (11-ounce) cans (312 gr) organic white corn, drained

3 green onions, chopped

2 beefsteak tomatoes, chopped

½ cup (120 ml) fresh cilantro (coriander), chopped

2 teaspoons fresh lime juice

1 ½ tablespoons homemade mayonnaise (see p. 204) or Delouis Fils brand

¼ teaspoon sea salt

Toss corn, onions, tomatoes, cilantro, and lime juice together in a large bowl. Stir in mayonnaise and season with salt. Refrigerate for 3 hours until very cold.

Napa Chicken Salad

The sweetness of the granola and grapes, crispness of the celery, and tang of the tomato and Gorgonzola is a satisfying combination that makes a delicious meal all on its own. **SERVES 4**

2 bone-in, skin-on, organic chicken breasts

Sea salt and freshly ground black pepper

8 cups (170 gr) mixed baby greens

15 grapes, red or green, cut in half

¼ cup (30 gr) unflavored granola

1 medium-size apple, cut into bite-size pieces (I prefer Braeburn and I leave the peel on)

1 stalk celery, chopped

¼ cup (25 gr) walnuts, chopped

1 ripe medium-size tomato, chopped

¼ to ½ cup (30 gr) crumbled Gorgonzola, in bite-size pieces

Salad Dressing:

4 tablespoons white wine vinegar

1 tablespoon honey

1 tablespoon maple syrup

2 tablespoons extra-virgin olive oil

Preheat oven to 425°F (220°C) and adjust rack to middle position.

Place chicken breasts in a roasting pan, skin side up, and season generously with salt and pepper. Roast chicken for 40 minutes until chicken is cooked through and skin is golden brown. Remove from oven and let cool completely. This step can be done in advance and the chicken kept in the fridge until you are ready to assemble the salad.

Toss greens, grapes, granola, apple, celery, walnuts, tomato, and Gorgonzola in a large salad bowl. Remove skin and bones from chicken, shred, and place on top of salad. Whisk together vinegar, honey, maple syrup, and olive oil in a small bowl and drizzle on top of the salad. Toss and serve immediately.

Wild Rice Thai Salad

The refreshingly light flavor of marinated mushrooms, hearty wild rice, vegetables, and herbs create a superb combination. If you have the time, let the salad sit at least two hours before serving because the longer it sits, the better it tastes.

SERVES 8

:::

Salad Dressing:

4 teaspoons fresh lime juice

6 tablespoons olive oil

2 tablespoons sesame oil

2 teaspoons honey

2 tablespoons soy sauce

2 tablespoons minced ginger

2 cloves garlic, minced

2 tablespoons spicy Asian chili sauce

5 ounces (140 gr) button mushrooms, cleaned and sliced

2 cups (400 gr, uncooked) wild rice, cooked according to package directions, then cooled

3 green onions, chopped

1 red bell pepper, cut into ½-inch (1.25 cm) pieces

Handful of basil, chopped

10 leaves of fresh mint, chopped

:::

Blend lime juice, olive oil, sesame oil, honey, soy sauce, ginger, garlic, and chili sauce in a blender until well combined. Put sliced mushrooms in a medium bowl and pour half of salad dressing over the top and toss. Let the mushrooms marinate in the dressing for 10 minutes.

Place prepared wild rice, green onion, and bell pepper in a large mixing bowl. Add marinated mushrooms, basil, mint, and remaining dressing. Toss until salad is thoroughly coated. Serve at room temperature.

Roasted Vegetable and Orzo Salad

Because you don't have to worry about keeping it cold, this is the perfect salad for BBQs and potlucks. The hearty orzo and the salty, savory vegetables topped with fresh herbs and tangy ricotta salata cheese pair wonderfully with juicy hamburgers or grilled chicken. **SERVES 8**

::

½ large red onion, cut into 1-inch pieces

1 large red pepper, cut into 1-inch (2.5 cm) pieces

1 large yellow pepper, cut into 1-inch (2.5 cm) pieces

2 zucchini, cut into 1-inch (2.5 cm) pieces

2 tablespoons coconut oil

Sea salt and freshly ground black pepper

½ pound (230 gr) whole wheat orzo (about 2 cups)

½ cup (120 ml) ricotta salata cheese, cut into small cubes

¼ cup (60 ml) chopped Kalamata olives

3 tablespoons chopped fresh basil

Salad Dressing:

2 tablespoons extra-virgin olive oil

1 tablespoon flaxseed oil (if not available, use extra-virgin olive oil)

3 tablespoons lemon juice

¼ teaspoon sea salt

⅛ teaspoon freshly ground black pepper

::

Preheat oven to 400°F (200°C) and adjust oven rack to middle position.

Toss red onion, red and yellow peppers, zucchini, and coconut oil together in a large bowl and spread out on a large baking sheet. Season generously with salt and pepper. Roast vegetables for about 30 minutes, stirring halfway through, until the vegetables are beginning to brown. Cool to room temperature.

Bring a large pot of water to boil and cook orzo al dente according to package directions. Rinse with cold water until the orzo is no longer warm. Pour orzo into a large bowl and toss with roasted vegetables, ricotta salata, and Kalamata olives.

Whisk together olive oil, flaxseed oil, lemon juice, and salt and pepper. Pour dressing over salad and toss until dressing is incorporated. Season to taste with additional salt and pepper, and stir in basil.

Serve at room temperature to enjoy the full flavor of the dressing. Keep in mind that the basil will wilt a bit, so add the basil just before serving.

Karin's Everyday Salad

Remember the hilarious story about my friend Karin in Chapter 1? Well, this is her salad that she let me modify. It's perfect on a warm summer night paired with chicken or fish, and a large hunk of homemade bread and butter. During the cooler months, you can exchange the tomato and cucumber with vegetables that are in season such as radishes and peppers. The beauty of this salad is that you mix everything in only one bowl. **SERVES 4**

8 cups (170 gr) mixed baby greens

2 carrots, peeled, cut into ¼-inch (6 mm) round slices

1 cucumber, skin removed, cut into ¼-inch (6 mm) round slices

2-3 medium tomatoes, roughly chopped

2-3 tablespoons lemon juice

2-3 tablespoons extra-virgin olive oil

1 tablespoon flaxseed oil (optional)

1 teaspoon dried Italian seasoning

2-3 tablespoons of freshly grated Pecorino Romano cheese

¼ teaspoon garlic powder

¾ teaspoon sea salt

⅛ teaspoon freshly ground black pepper

Toss mixed greens, carrots, cucumber, and tomatoes in a large mixing bowl. Add lemon juice, olive oil, flaxseed oil, Italian seasoning, grated cheese, garlic powder, salt, and pepper. Toss well.

VARIATION: Substitute arugula or spinach leaves for the baby greens.

Roasted Beet, Goat Cheese, and Sweet Pecan Salad

I created this salad while trying to incorporate more beets into my family's diet. Beets are a rich source of folic acid, vitamins A and C, and also have a stimulating effect on the liver's detoxifying process. In this family favorite that everyone requests, roasting the beets brings out their sweetness, and the tang from the goat cheese is a perfect complement. **SERVES 4**

2 medium-size beets, skins trimmed and sliced

1 tablespoon coconut oil

Sea salt

½ cup (60 gr) pecans, chopped

1 tablespoon maple syrup

3 cups (65 gr) mixed greens

¼ cup (30 gr) goat cheese, crumbled

Salad Dressing:

2 tablespoons balsamic vinegar

6 tablespoons extra-virgin olive oil

¼ teaspoon sea salt

¼ teaspoon freshly ground black pepper

Preheat oven to 400°F (200°C) and adjust rack to middle position.

Thinly slice the beets so the slices are about ¼-inch (6 mm) thick. Toss with coconut oil and season with salt. Place beets on baking dish in a single layer and roast for 15 minutes. Remove pan from oven and turn beets over, using a spatula. Roast for another 10 minutes and cool completely.

Lower oven temperature to 250°F (120°C). Toss pecans with the maple syrup and spread out on a baking sheet. Bake for 15 minutes, stir, then bake another 15 minutes until pecans are dried and crispy. Cool.

(The beets and pecans can be prepared earlier in the day and left at room temperature until you are ready to assemble the salad.)

To make the dressing, whisk balsamic vinegar, olive oil, salt, and pepper in a small bowl. Toss mixed greens with ¾ of the salad dressing. Add more dressing if needed. To assemble, divide salad greens on four plates. Divide the beets evenly and place on top of greens. Sprinkle with maple pecans and goat cheese. Serve immediately.

Butternut Squash, Pomegranate, and Roquefort Salad

My 8-year-old daughter and I created the concept of this salad one fall day at the grocery store when pomegranates and butternut squash were in season. She saw a squash and begged me to buy it so we could roast it at home—one of her favorite dishes. I told her we could but asked her how we could serve it differently. She looked around, saw a pomegranate, and said, "How about a salad?" So, I have my daughter to thank for this creation. **SERVES 4**

2 cups (475 ml) peeled bite-size pieces of butternut squash

1 tablespoon coconut oil

1 tablespoon whole cane sugar or Sucanat (see p. 18)

½ teaspoon sea salt

8 cups (170 gr) mixed baby greens

¼ cup (60 ml) pomegranate seeds

4 tablespoons crumbled Roquefort

1 teaspoon pomegranate juice

2 teaspoons balsamic vinegar

2 tablespoons extra-virgin olive oil

2 teaspoons maple syrup

Preheat oven to 400°F (200°C) and adjust rack to middle position.

Toss squash with coconut oil, whole cane sugar, and salt. Spread pieces evenly in a baking dish and cover with foil. Roast for 15 minutes, remove the foil, and then roast for an additional 20 minutes, until edges are golden brown. Remove from oven and cool.

Toss greens, pomegranate seeds, Roquefort, and cooled squash in a large bowl. Whisk together pomegranate juice, vinegar, olive oil, and maple syrup in a small bowl and drizzle over salad. Toss and serve immediately.

Side by Side

Helping Others Make the Change

- Remember, not everyone starts with the same base knowledge about food, so please be patient when helping someone who is making the shift to organic.

- Teach kids to read food labels. If they can't pronounce it, they should get adult advice before eating it.

- Bring kids into the kitchen while they are young and let them cook with you. A good starting point would be teaching them to make oatmeal (p. 52) and then progressing to more complicated dishes like scrambled eggs and toast.

- Share with friends the importance of coconut oil, butter, and other nourishing fats.

- Make a day of it with your friends at your local farmers market and ask farmers for their insights as to what's in season.

- Start a community garden with your neighbors and share tips and organic recipes. Together, you can cultivate anything from herbs to vegetables to fruits. Or, each neighbor can grow just a few items on the side of the house or backyard, which are then shared by all.

CHAPTER SIX

Sides

Sides

Jimmie's Cheesy Jalapeño Cornbread

This is an old-time favorite in our family. My grandma has been making this for years, and it reminds me of our summer visits to Baton Rouge, Louisiana, when I was a young girl. The jalapeños add a tangy touch of heat, but are completely optional. I usually make this bread half with jalapeños and half without to suit everyone's taste. While not technically a side, it's a great addition with gumbo, soups, and salads. **SERVES 8**

2 cups (300 gr) cornmeal, medium-fine grain

3 teaspoons baking powder

1 teaspoon sea salt

½ teaspoon baking soda

2 large eggs, lightly beaten

6 tablespoons unsalted butter, melted and cooled slightly

2 tablespoons coconut oil, melted and cooled slightly

1 cup (230 gr) sour cream or crème fraîche

1 cup (240 ml) corn kernels

2 teaspoons heavy cream

2 teaspoons organic whole cane sugar or Sucanat (see p. 18)

2 medium jalapeños, minced (optional)

⅓ cup (80 ml) yellow onion, minced

1 ½ cups (105 gr) grated Cheddar cheese

Preheat oven to 425°F (220°C) and adjust rack to middle position of oven. Butter an 8 x 8-inch (20 x 20 cm) baking dish.

Whisk cornmeal, baking powder, salt, and baking soda together in a large mixing bowl. In a separate bowl, whisk together the eggs, butter, coconut oil, and sour cream.

Pour corn, cream, and whole cane sugar into the bowl of a food processor. Pulse for about five 1-second pulses until combined. The corn should be roughly chopped.

Make a well in the middle of the dry ingredients. Add the wet ingredients, creamed corn from food processor, jalapeño peppers, and onion. Gently fold all ingredients together. Pour half of the cornbread batter into the baking dish and spread out evenly. Sprinkle the shredded cheese on top, and then pour the remaining batter on top. Bake for 30–35 minutes, or until the top is golden brown.

Spinach Madeline

This is one of my favorite holiday dishes. Even those who don't like spinach devour this dish because of its depth of flavor, creamy texture, and the spicy kick at the end. I hope it becomes one of your favorites, too. **SERVES 6**

2 (10-ounce) packages (560 gr) frozen chopped organic spinach, thawed

4 tablespoons unsalted butter

2 tablespoons whole wheat flour

2 tablespoons chopped yellow onion

¼ cup (60 ml) whole milk

¼ cup (60 ml) heavy cream

1 teaspoon Worcestershire sauce

1 teaspoon freshly ground black pepper

¾ teaspoon celery salt

½ teaspoon garlic powder

½ teaspoon sea salt

6 ounces (170 gr) Pepper Jack cheese, grated

Drain spinach and reserve ½ cup (120 ml) of the liquid. Melt butter over low heat in a medium saucepan. Whisk in flour and continue to whisk until blended but not brown. Stir in onion, and cook until soft. Whisk in reserved spinach juices, milk, and cream slowly, stirring constantly to avoid lumping. Stir in spinach. Cook until smooth and thick, about 3–4 minutes. Stir in Worcestershire sauce, black pepper, celery salt, garlic powder, salt, and Pepper Jack cheese. Stir until cheese is melted and seasonings are blended into mixture. Serve immediately.

 This dish can be frozen for up to three months.

Carrot Soufflé

Don't pass this one up. Unless you're from the South, you've probably never heard of this mildly sweet-tasting soufflé. You'd never know it's made from carrots. Please trust me when I say this will go on your most-requested list. Guests always ask for the recipe and often tell me later that it's now their child's new favorite. Although this recipe is intended to serve six, I am embarrassed to say on certain evenings it will only serve four. **SERVES 6**

1 pound (450 gr) carrots, peeled and cut into 1-inch (2.5 cm) pieces

¾ cup (180 ml) maple syrup

1 teaspoon vanilla extract (see p. 212)

1 teaspoon baking powder

2 tablespoons plus 1 teaspoon whole wheat pastry flour

½ teaspoon ground cinnamon

½ cup unsalted butter, melted

2 large eggs

Preheat oven to 350°F (180°C) and adjust rack to middle position. Butter an 8 x 8–inch (20 x 20 cm) baking dish.

Bring an inch of water to a simmer on medium-low heat in a medium saucepan. Add carrots, cover, and simmer for 15 minutes until tender. Drain well.

Pour cooked carrots into a food processor. Add maple syrup, vanilla, baking powder, flour, cinnamon, and melted butter, and puree. While the machine is running, add eggs one at a time through the tube. Process until smooth. Pour carrots into the pan. Bake for 1 hour or until set and edges are golden brown.

For additional color and texture when plated, you can bake this soufflé in buttered mini-muffin tins or ramekins, as shown to the right.

This dish freezes well. After puréeing, pour into a covered container and freeze. Thaw, pour into pan, and bake as stated above, when ready to use.

Fried Okra

This is my variation of the dish my mom used to introduce Southern, all-vegetable dinners to my Chicago-born, meat-and-potatoes dad. And, he loved it! In the summers, when okra was at its peak, Mom would make "fried" okra and serve it with big slices of Texas tomatoes, and a pot of black-eyed peas, and call it a meal. It doesn't get any more Southern than that. **SERVES 6**

4 cups (950 ml) fresh okra, cut into ½-inch (13 mm) rounds, ends discarded

1 medium yellow onion, minced

½ cup (75 gr) medium-to-fine ground cornmeal

2 teaspoons sea salt

4 tablespoons coconut oil

Toss okra, onion, cornmeal, and salt together in a large bowl. Heat large skillet over medium heat for 3 minutes. Add coconut oil to pan, swirling to coat. Pour okra mixture into skillet and stir every few minutes, for about 30 minutes, until golden brown.

Brussels Sprouts and Bacon Hash

Even if Brussels sprouts aren't your thing (you're not alone), this dish will change your mind. Salty bits of bacon and sweet caramelized onion tossed with steamed and chopped Brussels sprouts will have everyone coming back for seconds.

SERVES 4-6

::

1 pound (450 gr) small Brussels sprouts, cleaned, ends cut off

¾ cup (180 ml) water

½ teaspoon sea salt

6 slices of bacon, chopped (organic, nitrate-free and pastured preferred)

1 medium yellow onion, chopped

Sea salt

Freshly ground black pepper

::

Combine Brussels sprouts, water, and salt in a large saucepan. Bring to a boil, cover with lid, and lower heat to a simmer. Simmer for 8–10 minutes, until a knife inserted into a Brussels sprout goes in without any resistance. Drain Brussels sprouts and finely chop them.

Cook bacon over medium heat until crispy. Remove bacon with a slotted spoon. Drain grease until left with about 3 tablespoons. Add onion to pan and sauté in bacon fat until soft and caramelized, about 8 minutes. Add chopped Brussels sprouts and sauté with onions for 5 minutes. Add bacon, season with salt and pepper, and serve.

Mexican Rice Casserole

There are times when we all need a casserole that we know is reliable and has great flavor. I've taken this to many potlucks. It's simple enough to please the kids, but has enough depth of flavor to please adults. **SERVES 6-8**

::

2 poblano peppers

1 teaspoon coconut oil

1 cup (70 gr) grated Monterey Jack cheese

1 cup (70 gr) grated Cheddar cheese

4 cups (480 gr) cooked brown rice (see p. 207)

¼ cup (60 ml) cilantro (coriander), chopped

1 cup (240 ml) crème fraîche (see p. 200)

1 teaspoon ground cumin

½ teaspoon sea salt

::

Preheat broiler to high-heat setting and adjust rack so it sits just below broiler.

Coat peppers with coconut oil. Place peppers on baking sheet and put under broiler. Check the peppers after 2 minutes and broil until skin turns black and blistered. Turn peppers and broil until all sides are black and blistered. Take out of oven and immediately place in bowl with a lid. Uncover the chilies after 10 minutes and peel, seed and chop.

Preheat oven to 350°F (180°C) and adjust rack to middle position.

Stir together Monterey Jack and Cheddar in a small bowl. Stir together rice, 1 ½ cups (360 ml) of cheese mixture, cilantro, peppers, crème fraîche, cumin, and salt in a large bowl. Pour mixture into a greased baking dish and then top with remaining cheese. Bake for 30 minutes, or until mixture is bubbling and cheese is golden brown. Best served day prepared.

Buttermilk Mashed Potatoes

Years ago, while doing dishes after dinner, a friend asked me, "So, can you give me your recipe for mashed potatoes?" I laughed and naively thought she was joking. When I realized she wasn't, I was really embarrassed. We still laugh about it years later—especially because she never received the recipe. So Ginger, this one's for you. **SERVES 6-8**

3 pounds (1.4 kg) potatoes, preferably Yukon or red, rinsed and cut into 2-inch (5 cm) pieces
½ cup (120 ml) whole buttermilk (see p. 203)
¼ cup (60 ml) whole milk
½ cup (115 gr) unsalted butter
1 heaping tablespoon sour cream
Sea salt and freshly ground black pepper

Place potatoes in a large pot and add water to cover the potatoes by 1 inch (2.5 cm). Bring to a boil and cook until potatoes are fork tender. Drain.

While potatoes are cooking, heat buttermilk, milk, and butter in a medium saucepan over low heat until butter is melted.

Place potatoes back into pot and pour in milk mixture. Mash with a potato masher, stir in sour cream and season generously with salt and pepper.

Don't hold back—feel free to venture out and try different types of potatoes, like fingerlings when they're in season at the market. Purple potatoes are especially fun for kids.

Grilled Potatoes with Lemon Aioli

This recipe is great for any outdoor gathering for all ages. The potatoes can be boiled early in the day and set aside until you're ready to coat them with oil and put them on the grill. **SERVES 6**

3 pounds (1.4 kg) red baby potatoes, scrubbed and cut in half
2 tablespoons coconut oil
Sea salt and freshly ground black pepper

Lemon Aioli:
¼ cup (60 ml) homemade mayonnaise (see p. 204) or Delouis Fils brand
Juice from half a lemon
1 small clove garlic, minced
Pinch of sea salt

Place potatoes in a large pot and cover with water. Bring potatoes to a gentle boil and cook until a paring knife can pierce the potato easily, about 20 minutes. Drain potatoes and pour in a large baking dish.

Preheat grill on high for 10–15 minutes. Meanwhile, using a pastry brush, brush the flat side of each potato with coconut oil. Season generously with salt and pepper. Turn the grill down to medium-high and grill the potatoes flat-side-down until golden brown.

Whisk together the mayonnaise, lemon juice, garlic, and salt in a small bowl. Serve potatoes with aioli for dipping.

You may need to use a little bit more or less of the garlic depending upon the strength of the clove.

Sautéed Beets

This oft maligned vegetable is often overlooked as a possible staple in our diets. However, when sautéed with butter, it imparts a sweet and mild flavor. Choose beets whose roots are firm and deep in color, and the tops vibrant green. Beets are in their prime season June through October, although you can find them year-round at most grocery stores. **SERVES 4**

3 beets with tops (green leaves) attached
3 tablespoons unsalted butter
½ teaspoon sea salt
Freshly ground black pepper

Cut off stems and leaves and cut each beet in half. Place beets in large pot with water. Boil until the beets are tender, about 20 minutes. Remove beets, and after they have cooled a bit, peel them, and cut into small pieces. Chop up the leaves, discard stems.

In a large sauté pan, melt butter over medium heat. Add the beets, greens, and salt. Sauté for 3–4 minutes until the greens have wilted. Sprinkle a bit of cracked pepper on top.

Sautéed Summer Vegetables

I used to avoid Swiss chard until a friend made this recipe for me. Once I tasted it, I started incorporating this vegetable in my cooking. In this side, the sweetness of the coconut oil and carrots offsets the bitterness of the chard. When shopping for Swiss chard, look for stems that are crisp and freshly cut and leaves that are vibrant and glossy. **SERVES 6**

3 tablespoons coconut oil

3 leeks, thinly sliced crosswise, white parts only

2 red, yellow or orange bell peppers, sliced thin

4 carrots, peeled and shredded

2 zucchini, shredded

1 bunch red Swiss chard, chopped, tough stems discarded

4 tablespoons unsalted butter

1 teaspoon sea salt

⅛ teaspoon freshly ground black pepper

Heat coconut oil over medium-high heat in a large sauté pan. Add leeks and sauté until soft and just beginning to caramelize, about 8 minutes. Stir in the bell peppers and cook another 5 minutes, stirring every minute or so until slightly softened. Stir in carrots and zucchini and sauté 3–5 minutes. Add the Swiss chard and sauté until limp. Add the butter and stir the vegetables until the butter is melted. Season generously with salt and black pepper.

Be sure to clean leeks as follows: cut in half lengthwise and open up leeks to wash off any dirt residue.

Oven-Roasted Vegetables

Roasting vegetables in coconut oil brings out their sweetness, especially when it comes to cauliflower. This delicious blend of caramelized cauliflower, broccoli, and corn is the only way my kids will eat cauliflower. While we used to reach for the olive oil when roasting, remember that it's best to use coconut oil when cooking at a higher heat due to its high smoking point, as explained in Chapter 2 (see p. 20–21). **SERVES 6**

1 head cauliflower, cut into bite-size pieces

2 large crowns of broccoli, cut into bite-size pieces

3 cups (700 ml) corn kernels

¼ cup (60 ml) coconut oil, melted

2 teaspoons coarse sea salt

½ teaspoon freshly ground black pepper

Preheat oven to 400°F (200°C) and adjust rack to middle position.

Toss cauliflower, broccoli, corn, coconut oil, sea salt, and pepper in a large bowl and then spread out on a large baking sheet. Roast vegetables for about 30 minutes, stirring occasionally. Roast until the edges of the vegetables are golden brown. Serve immediately.

Grilled Halloumi with Oregano

A few years ago, a British couple was stationed with us at the same Air Force base. The wife, Sue, and I became dear friends. On one of our trips to the health food store, she introduced me to halloumi. This firm, salty cheese can be eaten straight out of the package and will hold its own on a grill. Kids usually call it "squeaky" cheese for the sound it makes when you bite into it. You can serve this dish, and the next two that follow, as a side or an appetizer. **SERVES 4**

1 (8-to-10-ounce) package halloumi cheese
Sea salt and freshly ground black pepper
1 tablespoon coconut oil
Extra-virgin olive oil, for drizzling
A few sprigs of oregano, chopped
Juice of half a lemon

Preheat grill on medium heat for 10 minutes. Slice halloumi in approximately ¼-inch (6 mm) thick slices and season with salt and pepper.

Dip a small paper towel wad in coconut oil and rub it on the grill's cooking grate to prevent cheese from sticking. Grill for 1–2 minutes per side, or until golden brown. Remove from the grill, drizzle with olive oil, sprinkle with oregano and lemon juice, and season with salt and pepper.

Sun-dried Tomato Hummus

Hummus is a favorite snack in our home. I usually make extra and keep it in the fridge for when we need a quick and healthy snack. It's great served with whole-grain pita, crackers, or as a spread on a sandwich. It keeps in the fridge for about two weeks. Enjoy it as a side or an appetizer. **MAKES 4 CUPS (960 ML)**

2 ¾ cups (660 ml) canned garbanzo beans, drained, liquid reserved

1 clove garlic, minced

½ cup (120 ml) tahini

3 tablespoons fresh lemon juice (approximately 1 lemon)

2 teaspoons coarse sea salt

½ teaspoon ground cumin

½ teaspoon paprika

2 tablespoons extra-virgin olive oil

¼ cup (60 ml) sun-dried tomatoes in olive oil, drained

Add all ingredients to a food processor and process about 3–4 minutes until all chunks are blended and the mixture is thick and creamy with a silky texture. If hummus is too thick, add ¼ to ½ cup (60–120 ml) of the reserved liquid. Adjust salt to taste.

 Tahini is sesame seed paste and can be found in most grocery stores.

Pete's Black Olive Pesto Dip

This easy black olive pesto dip is a mix of black olive pesto and cream cheese. No one can pass up spreading it on toasted bread or crackers when served bubbling hot from the oven. It was one of the first gourmet foods I introduced to my husband, and he even requested it for our wedding reception. **SERVES 10-12**

2 cups (475 ml) black olives, drained

1 cup (100 gr) walnuts

1 cup (100 gr) grated Pecorino Romano

¼ teapoon sea salt (optional)

2 cloves garlic

½ cup (120 ml) extra-virgin olive oil

8 ounces (230 gr) cream cheese, preferably cultured, room temperature

Whole wheat bread, preferably sourdough, sliced into small pieces and toasted, or crackers

Preheat oven to 350°F (180°C) and adjust rack to middle position.

Add olives, walnuts, Pecorino, salt, and garlic to a food processor or blender and process until smooth. With machine running, slowly add the olive oil until the pesto becomes smooth and thick.

Spread softened cream cheese evenly in the bottom of an oven-safe 8 x 8-inch (20 x 20 cm) dish. Pour pesto over cream cheese and spread on top evenly. Bake for 30 minutes, or until bubbling. Serve with toasted whole wheat sourdough or crackers.

This pesto freezes well. Just place in a freezer bag or container and it will keep for up to three months. You can also substitute basil or sun-dried tomatoes in place of the olives and serve over pasta. It also makes a wonderful condiment for an everyday turkey sandwich.

Organic Entrées

Points to Remember

- When you buy chicken, make sure it's organic, and preferably pastured or free range, which means the animal was given access to the outdoors and able to graze on pasture.

- Fish are only as clean as the water they swim in. So choose fish that were wild or ocean-caught—not farm-raised. Many farm-raised fish are fed fish meal that is made of ingredients such as animal by-products.

- My favorite budget-saving way to buy meat is to purchase it directly from the farmer. You not only know where your meat is coming from, the prices are lower than at the grocery store.

- If you buy organic beef at the grocery store, remember to buy certified organic. This means it is free of hormones, antibiotics, not irradiated, and fed only organic feed free of animal by-products.

- Each week, try replacing one of the non-organic ingredients in your pantry—even black pepper or salt—with an organic ingredient.

- Don't be surprised to find recipes that have saturated fats. As long as you eat these organic dishes in moderation, the saturated fats provide health benefits. The key is moderation.

CHAPTER SEVEN

Main Dishes

Main Dishes

Butterflied Chicken with Red Onions

This is a superb weeknight meal. After the chicken and onions go in the oven, I can tend to the kids, and then come back an hour later to toss a salad together. And, voila—this magnificent dinner is ready! **SERVES 4-6**

::

1 (4-5 pound) chicken (1.8-2.3 kg), butterflied
4 tablespoons unsalted butter, at room temperature
2-3 tablespoons fresh thyme
1 ½ teaspoons sea salt, divided
¼ teaspoon freshly ground black pepper
2 large red onions, cut into wedges
1 tablespoon coconut oil, melted

::

Preheat oven to 450°F (230°C) and adjust oven rack to medium position.

Pat chicken with a dry cloth to make sure the skin is dry. Stir together softened butter, thyme, and 1 teaspoon sea salt in a small bowl. Gently lift the skin and rub herbed butter under the skin of breasts, thighs, and legs. Season the entire chicken generously with salt and pepper.

Place chicken in roasting pan. Toss red onion wedges, coconut oil, remaining ½ teaspoon of sea salt, and pepper in a medium bowl. Pour onions around chicken in roasting pan. Roast chicken for 30 minutes and then rotate pan 180 degrees. Continue to roast, about 25 minutes, until crisp and golden brown, and when a thermometer reaches 160°F (70°C) when inserted in the thickest part of the breast. Remove from the oven and before serving, let the chicken rest for about 15 minutes to allow juices to redistribute.

 To butterfly the chicken, lay it breast side down. Using good kitchen shears, remove the backbone by cutting just to the left of the backbone all the way down the chicken and then repeat on the right side. Now remove. (Make sure to save the backbone for broth the next day.)

Egg Pasta with Truffle Oil

Fresh pasta with a creamy sauce is an elegant comfort food. I usually make this when I want something warm, quick, and soothing. The splash of truffle oil at the end adds an earthy tone that sends it over the top. **SERVES 4**

::

1 ½ cups (350 ml) cream

6 tablespoons unsalted butter

½ teaspoon sea salt

12 ounces (340 gr) fresh whole wheat linguine (see p. 198)

1 cup (100 gr) grated Pecorino Romano cheese

2–3 tablespoons black truffle oil

::

Heat cream, butter, and salt in a medium saucepan over low heat until steaming, about 10 minutes.

While sauce is heating, bring a large pot of salted water to a boil. Add egg pasta and cook until al dente, about 3–4 minutes. Scoop out the pasta with a pasta ladle and place it in the cream sauce. Stir in cheese and toss until the pasta absorbs the sauce.

Serve immediately, drizzling truffle oil on each serving. Sprinkle with extra grated cheese to taste.

Tuna Steaks with Avocado and Tomato Salsa

Fresh salsa over grilled tuna is a light and delicious meal. It's important to have the salsa ready before you grill the tuna steaks, which most people choose to cook rare for maximum flavor. If you haven't tried tuna rare or medium-rare, you'll be surprised at the depth of flavor, even if you prefer your beef medium or medium-well. We usually have everyone seated at the table while my husband cooks the steaks. He serves them immediately from the grill. **SERVES 4**

1 avocado, chopped

4 tomatoes, chopped

2 tablespoons minced red onion

1 clove garlic, minced

2 tablespoons minced parsley

1 tablespoon minced fresh oregano

1 tablespoon extra-virgin olive oil

1 teaspoon lemon juice

4 tuna steaks, about 1 ½-inches (4 cm) thick

3 tablespoons coconut oil

Sea salt and freshly ground black pepper

Gently toss avocado, tomato, red onion, garlic, parsley, oregano, olive oil, and lemon juice in a medium bowl.

Prepare a high-heat fire for your grill. Brush the tuna steaks with coconut oil and season both sides generously with salt and pepper. Grill steaks for 2 ½ minutes per side. Remove from heat and serve immediately with salsa spooned on top.

The grilling time is for rare tuna steaks. If you would like your steak medium-rare then cook 30 seconds longer on each side. Shop for tuna at a store you trust and that has a quick turn-around of its stock. The fish should be firm and smell like the ocean.

Tuscan Lemon Chicken

A few years ago on a trip to Italy, my parents went to a Florence restaurant known for its signature poultry dish. Mom enjoyed it so much that she asked the chef if she could see how it was prepared. It's not uncommon for Italian chefs to generously share their creations, which he did. Then Mom created her variation adding a light salad presentation on top. This is my organic version. **SERVES 4**

Chicken Cutlets:

1 ½ cups (225 gr) whole wheat flour

3 eggs, beaten

4 boneless, skinless chicken breasts, pounded to ½-inch (13 mm) thickness

½ teaspoon sea salt

½ teaspoon freshly ground black pepper

4 tablespoons unsalted butter

¼ cup (60 ml) extra-virgin olive oil

Salad:

2 tablespoons lemon juice

1 teaspoon Dijon mustard

½ teaspoon sea salt

½ teaspoon freshly ground black pepper

¼ cup (60 ml) extra-virgin olive oil

5 ounces (140 gr) baby romaine leaves

1 cup (165 gr) halved cherry or grape tomatoes

1 lemon, cut into wedges

Preheat oven to 300°F (150°C) and adjust oven rack to middle position.

Pour flour into a shallow pie plate. Pour the beaten eggs into another pie plate. Generously season both sides of each chicken breast with salt and pepper. Melt butter and olive oil in a large skillet over medium heat. While butter and oil heat, dip each chicken breast first in the flour, and then the eggs, and immediately place into hot pan.

Pan-fry chicken about 3 minutes per side, until each side is golden brown. Place a cooling rack on top of a large cookie sheet and lay chicken breasts on the rack, and place in the oven. Bake chicken for 7 minutes. You'll know the chicken is cooked through when a thermometer reads 160°F (70°C) when inserted into the thickest part of the breast.

Meanwhile, combine the lemon juice, mustard, salt, and pepper in a small bowl. Slowly pour in the olive oil while whisking constantly to emulsify the oil into the other ingredients. Place lettuce and tomatoes in a large salad bowl and toss with dressing.

To serve, place a chicken breast on each of the 4 plates. Squeeze a lemon quarter over each chicken breast and top the chicken with a healthy serving of the greens.

Grand Isle Shrimp

Grand Isle is a small island down at the tip of Louisiana. If you've never eaten this dish, *mes cheres*, you're in for a treat! This spicy shrimp dish can be assembled in the morning and left in the fridge until ready to bake. The seasoning is also excellent on other fish such as mahi-mahi and flounder. Simply mix the dry seasonings only and put in an empty spice jar. You'll now have your own organic Cajun seasoning available in the pantry. Be sure to serve Grand Isle Shrimp with a crusty loaf of bread to sop up the juices. Don't count on having leftovers. It's that good. **SERVES 4**

2 pounds (900 gr) 16-20 count shrimp, shell peeled to tail and deveined

2 tablespoons lemon juice

1 ½ teaspoons Herbamare (see p. 26)

2 tablespoons Worcestershire sauce

¾ teaspoon paprika

⅛ teaspoon cayenne pepper

1 ½ teaspoons garlic powder

½ cup (115 gr) unsalted butter, cut into pea-sized pieces

Preheat oven to 450°F (230°C) and adjust oven rack to middle position.

Place shrimp in a large cast-iron skillet in a single layer and sprinkle with lemon juice. I prefer a skillet because it conducts heat so well and allows you to cook the shrimp quickly. Cooking in a cast-iron skillet also gives a nice caramelized flavor and color to the shrimp. Season evenly with Herbamare, Worcestershire sauce, paprika, cayenne pepper, and garlic powder. Distribute butter evenly over shrimp.

Bake for 8 minutes. Serve immediately.

To devein shrimp, cut a small slit down the back of the tail and pull out the vein. Also, remember that healthy saturated fats in moderation can provide health benefits, as explained in Chapter 3.

Mustard Beer Chicken

This is the chicken recipe for the man in your life. Chicken, dredged in mustard and flour, pan fried, with a delicious beer sauce poured on top. Now, what guy wouldn't want this at the end of a long day? **SERVES 4**

:::

Chicken Cutlet:

4 tablespoons Dijon mustard

4 boneless, skinless chicken breasts

Sea salt and freshly ground black pepper

1 cup (150 gr) whole wheat flour

1 tablespoon dried oregano

3 tablespoons extra-virgin olive oil

3 tablespoons unsalted butter

Mustard Beer Sauce:

1 shallot, minced

2 cloves garlic, minced

2 tablespoons Dijon mustard

½ cup (120 ml) organic pale ale

¼ cup (60 ml) cream

¼ cup (60 ml) parsley, chopped

:::

Preheat oven to 400°F (200°C) and adjust rack to middle position.

Spread 1 tablespoon of mustard onto each chicken breast and season each breast with salt and pepper. Stir flour and oregano together in a shallow pie plate. Dredge chicken breasts in flour-oregano mixture.

Heat a large ovenproof skillet over medium heat for 2 minutes. Add olive oil and butter to pan, swirling to coat.

Place chicken in pan and cook until golden brown on the bottom side, about 3 minutes. Turn chicken over and sauté again until golden, another 3 minutes. Transfer chicken to a baking sheet topped with a cooling rack and put in the oven for 5 minutes, or until chicken registers 160 degrees (70°C) with a thermometer.

Put skillet with the drippings back on the stove over medium heat. Add the minced shallot and sauté until lightly browned. Add the garlic and sauté for 30 seconds and then stir in mustard and the ale. Bring the sauce to a simmer and scrape the bottom of the pan with a wooden spoon to get up all the brown bits. Remove the pan from the heat and stir in the cream. To serve, ladle sauce over chicken and top with chopped parsley.

Oven-Roasted Wings

I first had these wings at my parents' home on Super Bowl Sunday. The guys were glued to the TV screen while Mom and I prepared her sticky, spicy wings recipe. I've tweaked her recipe to create these oven-roasted wings. They're completely addicting. **SERVES 6-8**

½ cup (60 gr) unsalted butter

1 cup (185 gr) whole cane sugar or Sucanat (see p. 18)

½ cup (120 ml) red wine

½ cup (120 ml) soy sauce

¼ cup (60 ml) fresh lemon juice

2 teaspoons Dijon mustard

4 tablespoons hot sauce

4-5 pounds (1.8-2.3 kg) chicken wings

2 teaspoons sea salt

¼ teaspoon black pepper

2 teaspoons garlic powder

Preheat oven to 350°F (180°C) and adjust rack to middle position.

Melt butter in a medium saucepan and add the cane sugar, wine, soy sauce, lemon juice, mustard, and hot sauce. Whisk all ingredients until combined and dissolved. (The sauce at this point will be very thin but it will thicken as it cooks.) Pour sauce over wings and season with salt, pepper, and garlic powder.

Bake wings for 35-40 minutes. Reduce heat to 250°F (120°C) and continue baking for 4–5 hours. Check and stir 3–4 times while baking, turning over wings when stirring. When wings are ready, the sauce will be very thick and syrupy.

Beef and Broccoli Stir-Fry

When I was a kid in suburban Dallas, it was a treat to eat at Cathy's Wok & Grill, owned by Catherine Liu, a dear family friend. The author of *Chinese Cooking the American Way,* she taught the finer art of Chinese cooking to such notables as Stanley Marcus, of Neiman Marcus fame, and Itzhak Perlman, the famed Israeli violinist. This is my version of this classic recipe, which I often ordered. If it's going to be a busy day, I'll prep the ingredients in the morning so when I come home I can have dinner on the table in about 15 minutes. **SERVES 4-6**

Steak Marinade:

1½ pounds (680 gr) sirloin, sliced thin, against the grain (as noted on p. 74)

1 tablespoon soy sauce

1 tablespoon sherry

Ginger and Garlic Mixture:

2 cloves garlic, minced

1 tablespoon minced ginger

1 teaspoon coconut oil

Garlic Sauce:

3 tablespoons sherry

3 tablespoons chicken broth

3 tablespoons soy sauce

½ teaspoon sesame oil

2 cloves garlic, minced

1 teaspoon arrowroot

1 teaspoon honey

3 tablespoons coconut oil, divided

1 ½ pounds (680 gr) broccoli, cut into bite-size pieces

3 carrots, diagonally sliced into thin coins

1 large red, orange or yellow bell pepper, cut into thin slices

1 recipe brown rice (see p. 207)

Toss together the sirloin, soy sauce and sherry in a small bowl. Whisk the garlic, ginger, and 1 teaspoon of the coconut oil in a small bowl. Whisk together sherry, chicken broth, soy sauce, sesame oil, garlic, arrowroot, and honey in another small bowl. Pour 2 tablespoons of water in a small bowl and set near the stove along with a lid for your skillet. (If you don't have a lid, use a few pieces of foil.)

Heat a large skillet over medium-high heat for 2 minutes. Add 2 tablespoons of coconut oil to pan and swirl to coat. Place sirloin in one single layer in skillet and don't stir. Cook sirloin for about 1 minute until bottom side is brown. Turn, using tongs, and cook until brown on the bottom, about 1 minute. Transfer sirloin to a clean bowl.

Add remaining 1 tablespoon of coconut oil to now empty skillet and heat until just shimmering. Add broccoli and carrots. Stir continuously for about 1 minute. Add 2 table-spoons of water and quickly cover skillet with lid. Leave lid on skillet for about 30 seconds. Remove lid, add bell peppers and let cook, stirring continuously, until all of the water has evaporated.

Make a well in the center of the vegetables and add the ginger-and-garlic mixture. Stir ginger and garlic in the middle of the pan for about 45 seconds and then combine with the rest of the vegetables. Add sirloin slices and garlic sauce to pan. Toss until sauce begins to thicken and ingredients are well coated. Serve immediately over brown rice.

Beef Stroganoff

Beef stroganoff brings back memories of being a kid in the '80s. Instead of noodles, my mom ladled her stroganoff over baked potatoes. The dish went out of vogue for a while, but I think it deserves a place on the table. Thinly sliced sirloin served in a rich, creamy sauce and poured over egg noodles is the perfect comfort meal on cold winter days. When possible, buy grass-fed beef, which is naturally higher in omega-3 fatty acids and CLAs (conjugated linoleic acid). Properly raised, grass-fed beef can be just as tender as conventionally raised choice cuts. **SERVES 4**

Sea salt and freshly ground black pepper

1 pound (450 gr) sirloin

4 tablespoons coconut oil, divided

12 ounces (340 gr) button mushrooms, cleaned and sliced

1 cup (340 ml) chicken broth, divided

1 tablespoon unsalted butter

1 medium yellow onion, finely chopped

1 teaspoon tomato paste

1 teaspoon whole cane sugar or Sucanat (see p. 18)

1 tablespoon whole wheat flour

½ cup (120 ml) white wine

⅓ cup (77 gr) sour cream, cultured preferred

8 ounces (230 gr) egg noodles, cooked and drained

Generously salt and pepper both sides of sirloin and then cut into thin strips against the grain at a sharp 45-degree angle. (Remember, sirloin has distinct lines, or striations, in it. If you cut with the grain, the meat won't be as tender.)

Heat 2 tablespoons coconut oil in a large sauté pan. Sauté mushrooms over medium heat until the edges are golden brown and they have lost most of their moisture, about 10–12 minutes. Season the mushrooms with salt and pepper and then pour into a large bowl.

Using the same pan, add remaining 2 tablespoons of coconut oil. Lay sirloin pieces in a single layer and brown the sirloin on each side. Be careful not to overcrowd the pan or they will not brown. Transfer meat to the bowl with the mushrooms and then repeat until all of meat is browned.

Pour ½ cup (120 ml) of chicken broth into the pan. Scrape all of the brown bits up from the bottom of the pan and bring the broth to a simmer. Simmer until broth is reduced by half. Pour broth into the bowl with the mushrooms and meat.

Return the skillet to the stove over medium-low heat. Melt the butter. After foaming subsides, add the onion, tomato paste, and cane sugar. Sauté for about 6 minutes until the onion turns golden brown. Stir in the flour and stir constantly for about 30 seconds. Add the remaining ½ cup (120 ml) broth and the white wine. Bring sauce to a boil and then reduce to a simmer for 2 minutes.

Spoon sour cream into a small bowl. Add half a cup of the sauce to the sour cream and stir. (This will keep the sour cream from curdling.) Add the sour cream mixture to the pan, along with the beef and mushrooms. Stir until thoroughly combined. Season with salt and pepper to taste. Serve over egg noodles.

Spinach and Herb Risotto

There is nothing better at the end of a long day than sitting down to a bowl of risotto and a glass of wine. The pesto in this dish imparts an unique flavor to this classic. This recipe was adapted from Alan Tardi's recipe in *Fine Cooking* magazine.

SERVES 4-6

¾ cup (60 gr) spinach, stems removed

¼ cup (60 ml) chopped parsley

1 tablespoon chopped fresh thyme

2 tablespoons grated Pecorino Romano cheese

3 cups (700 ml) plus 2 tablespoons chicken stock, preferably homemade (see p. 206), divided

3 tablespoons unsalted butter, divided

1 ½ cups (200 gr) brown Arborio rice or brown short-grain rice

½ cup (120 ml) minced yellow onion

½ cup (120 ml) dry white wine

Sea salt and freshly ground black pepper

Place spinach, parsley, thyme, cheese, and 2 tablespoons chicken stock in a food processor and process until coarsely chopped. Transfer to a medium saucepan and bring to a simmer. Turn to low heat to keep hot.

In another medium saucepan, melt 2 tablespoons of the butter over medium-high heat. Add the rice and stir for about 30 seconds until the rice is coated in butter. Add the onion and cook until translucent, about 1–2 minutes. Add the wine, stir, and simmer until almost all of the liquid has disappeared. Add just enough stock to cover the top of the rice. Lower the heat to maintain a low boil or vigorous simmer and stir frequently until rice absorbs liquid. When the stock is almost gone, add more stock to cover the rice and stir. Repeat this process 2–3 more times until the rice is just al dente. Add the remaining 1 tablespoon of butter and then stir in the spinach pesto. The risotto should be very creamy. Serve immediately.

 I prefer Frey Vineyards' organic, sulfite-free wine.

Southwestern Grilled Chicken

Here is a great recipe to whip up quickly after a day at work. The night before, you can marinate the chicken, prepare the salsa, and store everything in the fridge. All you have to do is fire up the grill, top the chicken with avocado and cheese, and serve with salsa. **SERVES 4**

Marinated Chicken:

3 tablespoons cider vinegar

¼ cup (60 ml) extra-virgin olive oil

1 tablespoon Dijon mustard

½ teaspoon dried dill

½ teaspoon dried basil

Sea salt and freshly ground black pepper

4 boneless, skinless chicken breasts

1 avocado, thinly sliced

4 ounces (115 gr) Monterey Jack cheese, cut into thin slices

Salsa:

½ medium red onion, diced

2 ripe tomatoes, chopped

2 cloves garlic, minced

½ medium jalapeño, seeded and minced

¼ cup (60 ml) cilantro, chopped

2 tablespoons lime juice (about 1 lime)

½ teaspoon sea salt

Whisk cider vinegar, oil, mustard, dill, basil, salt, and pepper in a small mixing bowl. Place chicken in a large bowl and pour marinade over. Cover and marinate overnight. Or, if you're short on time, marinate 1 hour at room temperature.

Place red onion, tomatoes, garlic, jalapeño, cilantro, lime juice, and sea salt in the bowl of a food processor and pulse 3–4 times. Pour salsa into a small bowl (can be made a day ahead).

Preheat the grill on medium-high for 15 minutes. Preheat your oven's broiler. Grill each piece of chicken about 6 minutes per side until cooked through. Top each piece of chicken with 2–3 avocado slices and 1–2 slices of cheese. Place under the broiler until melted, about 1 minute. Serve with salsa.

Cottage Pie

We can always add a dish like this cottage pie to our repertoire of hearty comfort food. The ground beef is sautéed with vegetables and herbs and topped with a cheesy, mashed potato crust to produce a satisfying dinner. When the pie comes out, piping hot with the cheese bubbling and browned, you'll have a hard time waiting to take the first bite! **SERVES 4-6**

Meat Filling:

½ cup (120 ml) breadcrumbs

⅓ cup (80 ml) heavy cream

2 tablespoons extra-virgin olive oil

½ red bell pepper, finely chopped

½ medium onion, finely chopped

1 stalk celery, finely chopped

1 carrot, finely chopped

¾ teaspoon sea salt

¼ teaspoon freshly ground black pepper

½ teaspoon dried thyme

1 pound (450 gr) ground beef

Potato Layer:

3 pounds (1.4 kg) potatoes, preferably Yukon or red, rinsed and cut into 2-inch pieces

½ cup (115 gr) unsalted butter

½ cup (120 ml) buttermilk (see p. 203)

1 heaping tablespoon sour cream

¼ cup (60 ml) milk

1 ½ cups (110 gr) grated Cheddar cheese, divided

1 tablespoon coarse sea salt

Freshly ground black pepper

Preheat oven to 350°F (180°C) and adjust oven rack to medium position. Combine breadcrumbs and cream in a large bowl.

Heat the olive oil in a large skillet over medium heat. Add the bell pepper, onion, celery, and carrot and sauté the vegetables until tender, about 5 minutes. Make a well in the center of the vegetables and add the salt, pepper, and thyme. Stir the seasonings in the middle of the pan until fragrant, about 30 seconds, and then stir into the vegetables. Add the ground beef and stir and cook until beef is partially cooked, about 5–7 minutes. Pour the beef filling into the bowl with breadcrumbs and stir until combined. Pour into a 13 x 9-inch (33 x 22 cm) baking dish and spread evenly into a single layer.

Fill a large stockpot with water and add potatoes. Boil the potatoes until tender. Drain in a colander. Put stockpot back on stove over low heat. Add the butter. When butter is melted add buttermilk (see p. 203), sour cream, milk, potatoes, and 1 cup (70 gr) of cheese. Mash the potatoes with a potato masher and then season with salt and pepper. Spread potatoes over beef layer in baking dish. Sprinkle with remaining ½ cup (35 gr) Cheddar cheese. Bake for 30 minutes or until bubbling and cheese is golden brown. Let cool for 5 minutes before serving.

 To make homemade breadcrumbs, simply put a few pieces of whole grain bread in the food processor and process until fine. You can keep extras in a sealed container in the freezer for up to three months.

Spicy Black Bean Soup

I love this tempting twist on black bean soup. The jalapeño gives it a kick while the sour cream gives it a light creamy texture. **SERVES 6**

::

2 cups (400 gr) black beans, soaked overnight, then drained

8 cups (1.9 liters) beef stock

1 (28-ounce) can (795 gr) diced tomatoes

1 teaspoon paprika

1 teaspoon onion powder

1 teaspoon garlic powder

1 heaping tablespoon coarse sea salt

1 tablespoon tomato paste

½ bunch cilantro, chopped, plus 2-3 tablespoons more for garnish

1 large jalapeño, seeded and sliced (use 1 ½ jalapeños if you prefer a spicier soup)

1 bunch green onions, chopped

4 tablespoons sour cream

::

Combine beans, stock, tomatoes, paprika, onion powder, garlic powder, sea salt, and tomato paste in large pot. Bring to a boil and then lower heat and simmer for 3 hours, until beans are tender.

Add cilantro, jalapeño, and green onions to soup and let simmer for 5 minutes. Using a hand immersion blender, blend until smooth, or transfer to a blender in batches and blend until smooth. Serve with a dollop of sour cream and sprinkle with cilantro.

Turkey and Brie Panini

A few years ago I really got into making panini sandwiches. At the time I didn't have a panini press, so I used a grill pan and pressed my sandwiches with a pot. I love making them because I can substitute whatever meats, vegetables, cheese, or other ingredients I have on hand to produce a dish that will impress any friend who walks through my door. **SERVES 4**

1 loaf good quality sourdough bread

Softened unsalted butter for spreading

¼ cup (60 ml) raspberry jam

½ pound (230 gr) thinly sliced turkey

1 cup (30 gr) arugula

6 ounces (170 gr) Brie, sliced

Slice 8 pieces of bread to about ¼-inch (6 mm) thickness. Butter 1 side of each piece of bread. Spread a thin layer of raspberry jam on the unbuttered side of 1 slice. Layer it with turkey, a few leaves of arugula, and a few slices of Brie. Top with another slice of bread, unbuttered side down.

Heat in a panini press, grill pan, or skillet until both sides are golden brown and cheese has melted inside.

It is best to buy your sourdough bread from an artisan bakery which usually uses a longer fermentation process, as this adds more flavor and nutritional value.

Chicken and Black Bean Quesadillas

These quesadillas are a quick, wonderful any-time-of-day meal. As a family, we eat them more often than sandwiches, occasionally even for breakfast. Whenever I leave town, I make sure I have the black bean spread and lots of tortillas and cheese in the fridge because my husband will live on them for days. **SERVES 6-8**

Chicken Marinade:

2 boneless, skinless chicken breasts

2 tablespoons lime juice, about 1 lime

2 tablespoons red wine vinegar

¼ cup (60 ml) extra-virgin olive oil

2 cloves garlic, minced

Sea salt and freshly ground black pepper

Black Bean Spread:

1 (15-ounce) can (245 gr) black beans, drained

Juice of 1 lime

1 teaspoon garlic powder

¼ teaspoon sea salt

8 ounces (230 gr) Cheddar cheese, grated, about 1 cup (240 ml)

8 ounces (230 gr) Monterey Jack cheese, grated, about 1 cup (240 ml)

Juice of 1 lime

¼ cup (60 ml) cilantro, chopped

8 whole wheat tortillas, preferably Ezekiel sprouted grain

Place chicken in a large bowl. Add the lime juice, vinegar, olive oil, garlic, salt, and pepper and toss until chicken is coated well. Marinate at room temperature for 1 hour. Grill or broil chicken for 4 minutes on each side, or until a thermometer reads 160°F (70°C) when inserted into thickest part of breast. Tent with foil.

Shred the chicken when cool enough to handle. (Shredded chicken can be prepared a day or two in advance and kept in the refrigerator, or store the cooked and shredded breasts in a covered container in the freezer for up to 3 months.)

Pour beans, lime juice, garlic powder, and salt into the food processor and process until smooth. Toss cheeses, lime juice, and cilantro in large bowl.

Place 4 of the tortillas on a flat work surface. Spread a thin layer of beans on each tortilla, sprinkle with cheese and top with shredded chicken. Make sure not to put the cheese too close to the outside of the tortillas to prevent it from oozing out.

Heat a large skillet over medium heat. Place 1 quesadilla in the skillet and cook until golden brown, about 1 minute. Flip quesadilla and cook until bottom is golden brown and cheese is melted. Serve alone or with some salsa or a generous dollop of guacamole.

For a more smoky flavor, grill the quesadillas over medium heat for 2 minutes per side.

The black bean spread will keep in the fridge for about two weeks and is perfect for late-night nachos. For salsa, you can use the recipe found on p. 140.

Roasted Jalapeño Hamburgers

My family loves burgers. On Sundays after church, we often enjoy eating grilled hamburgers. My husband created this "secret" recipe when we challenged one another to a hamburger face-off one afternoon. I think we all won. **SERVES 4**

2 medium jalapeños

1 pound (450 gr) beef

1 teaspoon Herbamare seasoning (see p. 25)

4 tablespoons homemade mayonnaise (see p. 204) or Delouis Fils brand

4 whole wheat hamburger buns

½ avocado, cut into slices

4 slices tomato

4 slices Pepper Jack cheese

Preheat broiler on high. Place jalapeños on baking sheet and broil 2–3 minutes until skin blackens. Turn jalapeños and continue to cook on second side until skins blacken. Remove from oven and quickly place in a bowl and cover tightly with plastic wrap. Let sit for 10 minutes. Remove plastic wrap and peel skin off jalapeños. Cut pepper in half, remove the seeds, and then cut into small slices.

Divide meat into 4 portions. Sprinkle a generous amount (about ¼ teaspoon) of Herbamare on each portion. Gently massage seasoning into meat. Flatten each portion to ¾-inch (1.9 cm) thick patty. Gently press center of patty down to create a slight depression, about ½-inch (1.3 cm) diameter. Lightly sprinkle the patty again with Herbamare. Grill burger to desired doneness.

Spread 1 tablespoon mayonnaise on each bun. Lay each bun flat-side-down on cooler part of grill and cook until lightly brown (this only takes about 1 minute). Heat your oven's broiler.

To assemble burgers, place jalapeño slices on patty and top with avocado, tomato, and cheese. Place under broiler until melted, about 1 minute. Place hamburger patties on buns and serve.

Chicken Scampi with Angel Hair Pasta

This is an easy-to-prepare dish and great for serving guests. Pair this with a large mixed green salad, fresh whole wheat bread, and you're ready to go. **SERVES 4**

::

Chicken Cutlets:

4 boneless, skinless chicken breasts, pounded to ½-inch (1.3 cm) thickness

1 teaspoon sea salt

½ teaspoon freshly ground black pepper

1 teaspoon dried oregano

½ cup (65 gr) whole wheat pastry flour (see p. 23)

3 tablespoons extra-virgin olive oil

3 tablespoons unsalted butter

Pasta Sauce:

2 tablespoons unsalted butter, divided

1 tablespoon extra-virgin olive oil

½ cup (120 ml) minced shallots

1 tablespoon minced garlic

¼ cup (60 ml) frozen artichoke hearts, thawed, roughly chopped

1 roasted yellow bell pepper, chopped

¼ cup (60 ml) sun-dried tomatoes in oil, chopped

2 tablespoons lemon juice

½ cup (120 ml) chicken broth

2-3 tablespoons white wine

Sea salt and freshly ground black pepper

1 pound (450 gr) whole wheat angel hair pasta, cooked and drained

¼ cup (60 ml) parsley, chopped

::

Season chicken breasts on both sides with salt, pepper, and dried oregano. Pour flour in a shallow pie plate and lightly coat each piece of chicken in flour.

Heat a large skillet over medium heat for 2 minutes. Add olive oil and butter to the pan. When foaming subsides, add chicken and brown on each side until cooked through, about

3 minutes per side. You'll know the chicken is cooked through when a thermometer reads 160°F (70°C) when inserted into the thickest part of the breast. Remove chicken from pan and tent loosely with foil.

Add 1 tablespoon of the butter and the 1 tablespoon oil to the skillet with the drippings. Add minced shallots and sauté until soft, about 3–4 minutes. Add the garlic and sauté for 20–30 seconds. Immediately stir in the artichoke hearts, yellow pepper, sun-dried tomatoes, and lemon juice. Cook 3–4 minutes, until flavors meld and vegetables are heated through, stirring occasionally.

Add chicken broth and wine, bring to a simmer, and continue to simmer for 3–4 minutes. Add remaining tablespoon of butter and season sauce with salt and pepper to taste. Place chicken back into pan with sauce and cook for 1–2 minutes, until heated through. Serve over angel hair pasta. Top with chopped parsley.

For a gluten-free option, dredge the chicken in rice flour and use rice pasta. My favorite is Tinkyada.

Loaded Baked Potato Soup

This is the perfect soup for a cold wintry day. It's wholesome, creamy, buttery, and will warm you up from the inside out. Both adults and kids devour this soup!

SERVES 6

½ cup (115 gr) unsalted butter, divided

2 cups (475 ml) chopped celery

2 cups (240 gr) chopped carrots

2 cups (320 gr) chopped yellow onion

4 cups (950 ml) Yukon potatoes, cut into
1 ½-inch (3.8 cm) pieces

8 cups (1.9 liter) chicken stock (see p. 206)

1 cup (240 ml) cream

1 teaspoon sea salt

½ cup (65 gr) whole wheat pastry flour

½ cup (35 gr) grated Cheddar cheese

¼ cup (58 gr) sour cream

3 green onions, chopped

Melt ¼ cup (60 ml) butter in a Dutch oven over low heat. Add celery, carrots, and onions, and stir to combine. Cover and cook for 30 minutes. When vegetables are tender, add potatoes and chicken stock and stir. Increase heat to high and bring to a boil. Lower heat and simmer 30 minutes, until vegetables are tender. Stir in cream and salt and heat until steaming.

Melt remaining ¼ cup (60 ml) butter in a small saucepan. The butter will foam after about a minute. Whisk in flour and cook for a few minutes, stirring constantly, until thickened. Add to the soup. Puree with a hand immersion blender until smooth and creamy, or blend the soup in a blender in small batches until smooth. Adjust spices to taste. Garnish with cheese, sour cream, and green onions.

I always leave the skins on the potatoes because the skins provide the enzymes to help your body digest the flesh of the potato. The end product is a bit more rustic in color but provides necessary nutrients.

Stove Top Macaroni and Cheese

I know we all love the idea of boxed macaroni and cheese, but let's be honest. The processed ingredients aren't the most nutritious. So, here's a healthier, quick stove top mac and cheese that you can have on the table in less than 15 minutes.

SERVES 6-8

:::

1 pound (450 gr) small rice pasta shells

½ cup (115 gr) unsalted butter

1 ½ cups (355 ml) milk

1 tablespoon arrowroot

1 teaspoon sea salt

¼ teaspoon freshly ground black pepper

12 ounces (290 gr) Cheddar cheese, grated

:::

Bring a large pot of salted water to a boil. Add pasta shells and cook until al dente, according to package directions. Drain the pasta in a colander.

Return the pot to the stove over medium-low heat. Melt the butter in the pot and then add the milk, arrowroot, salt, and pepper. Whisk sauce until thoroughly combined and then add the pasta back to the pot. Top with the cheese. Stir until the cheese is melted and the pasta is thickly coated with cheese. Serve immediately.

Louisiana Chicken Gumbo

My mom is from Louisiana so I grew up eating lots of Cajun food. I've always loved a good cup of gumbo so I came up with this recipe by combining some of the elements from my mom and grandma's gumbo recipes. The filé (found in the spice aisle at your local grocery store) adds a nice depth at the end of the dish. This gumbo is perfect for serving crowds, and it freezes very well. **SERVES 6**

½ cup (115 gr) butter

½ cup (75 gr) whole wheat flour

2 medium cloves garlic, minced

2 medium yellow onions, finely chopped

3 stalks celery, finely chopped

1 large green bell pepper, finely chopped

16 ounces (450 gr) okra, chopped

1 (3-4 pound) chicken (1.4–1.8 kg), cut up

3 large tomatoes, chopped

1 tablespoon tomato paste

½ cup (120 ml) white wine (optional)

1 ½ tablespoons sea salt, plus more to taste

¼ teaspoon cayenne pepper

½ teaspoon dried thyme

2 bay leaves

½ teaspoon dried oregano

Freshly ground black pepper

1 recipe brown rice (see p. 207)

Filé powder for sprinkling

Melt butter over medium-high heat in a large stockpot until foaming subsides, about 1 minute. Slowly add flour, whisking constantly until it becomes a deep mahogany color, 5–7 minutes. Stir in garlic, onion, celery, and bell pepper until vegetables are softened, about 5 minutes. Stir in okra. Sauté, stirring occasionally until vegetables look like melted Nestle's Crunch bars (as my mom would say), about 15 minutes.

Add chicken, 8 cups (1.9 liters) water, tomatoes, tomato paste, white wine, salt, cayenne, thyme, bay leaves, and oregano. Stir to combine. Turn heat to high and bring to a boil. Reduce temperature to medium-low and simmer for about 1 hour, or until chicken is cooked through.

Pull chicken pieces from the pot. When cool, pull off the bone, discard the skin, shred, and add shredded chicken back to the pot. Remove bay leaves. Adjust seasonings to taste with sea salt and pepper.

Serve gumbo over brown rice and sprinkle on top with filé to taste.

Three generations, one love for cooking.

On the left is my grandmother, Jimmie Brice, who was born in Baton Rouge, Louisiana. She is the author of *Cooking With Louisiana Baptists*, which has many gems from the countless church potlucks where my grandfather, Rev. Thurston Brice, was the pastor. My mother, Sandy Korem, is holding her company's collection of prized recipes, which inspired some of the recipes in this book. Mom nurtured my enthusiasm for cooking and sharing with others, which eventually led to this cookbook.

Grandma's Crawfish Étouffée

My grandmother really knows how to make étouffée, a cherished Louisiana tradition, which she passed on to my mom. My mom served this dish in a large soup crock in the middle of the table with plenty of buttered sourdough to sop up any remaining savory sauce from our bowls. This lunch or dinner specialty is best served with buttered whole wheat sourdough bread and a fresh salad. **SERVES 6**

1 ¾ sticks (200 gr) plus 3 tablespoons unsalted butter, divided

2 medium yellow onions, chopped

1 green pepper, chopped

1 rib celery, chopped

6 tablespoons chopped garlic, divided

2 pounds (900 gr) crawfish tails

1 pound (450 gr) cremini mushrooms, chopped

¾ teaspoons sea salt plus more to taste

⅛ teaspoon freshly ground black pepper plus more to taste

3 tablespoons whole wheat flour

1 ½ cups (350 ml) chicken stock (see p. 206)

1 ½ cups (350 ml) cream

1 teaspoon paprika

2-3 dashes cayenne pepper

1 recipe brown rice (see p. 207)

½ cup green onions

Melt 1 ¾ sticks (200 gr) butter in a large pot over medium heat. When foaming subsides, add onion, pepper, and celery. Sauté until vegetables are softened, 6–8 minutes. Stir in 3 tablespoons garlic and cook for 1 minute. Add 1 cup (240 ml) of water and the crawfish tails. Lower heat to medium-low and cook for 10 minutes, until crawfish is cooked through.

While crawfish is cooking, melt remaining 3 tablespoons of butter in a medium saucepan. Stir in mushrooms, remaining 3 tablespoons garlic, salt, and pepper. Cook until mushrooms have released their moisture, about 5–7 minutes. Add flour while continuously stirring and cook for about 30 seconds to cook the flour. Stir in stock and cream and simmer until sauce is thick and reduced, about 12 minutes.

Add creamed mushrooms to crawfish. Add paprika and cayenne pepper and stir. Season to taste with salt and pepper.

Serve étouffée over a bed of brown rice and garnish with green onions.

 If fresh crawfish isn't available, then frozen crawfish or shrimp make great substitutes.

Red Beans and Rice

When the scents of red beans and rice, a Louisiana staple, waft through the house, they say "home" to me. I usually put the beans and sausage on the stove late in the morning and let them slowly simmer through the day so the aroma of sausage and garlic permeates the house. This dish freezes extremely well (minus the rice) and always tastes better the second day. **SERVES 6**

4 cups (900 gr) dried kidney beans

1 (28-ounce) can (795 gr) diced tomatoes

1 tablespoon garlic powder

1 tablespoon sea salt

12 ounces (340 gr) of organic sausage, sliced into coins

1 recipe brown rice (see p. 207)

The night before, pour beans into a large bowl and cover with water. Leave at room temperature overnight. The next day, drain the beans and pour them into a large stockpot. Cover the beans with water and stir in the tomatoes, garlic powder, sea salt, and sausage. Bring to a boil, skim any scum off the top, and turn the temperature down to low. Cover and simmer for about 3 hours, until beans are tender. Add more salt or garlic powder to taste and serve over rice.

Substitute four 15-ounce (850 gr) cans of organic kidney beans for dried beans. Rinse them well before using. For an extra kick at the table, add a few splashes of organic hot sauce.

Chicken Curry

While living in the California desert, my friend Priya made this curry for her son's birthday party and everyone oohed and aahed over it. Who knew I would taste amazing curry on an Air Force base in the "Exact Center of Nowhere"? Priya was kind enough to share her recipe with me. **SERVES 6**

3 pounds (1.4 kg) boneless, skinless chicken breasts, cut into 1-inch (2.5 cm) pieces

Yogurt Marinade:

1 cup (240 ml) plain whole yogurt

1 teaspoon tikka masala (an Indian spice blend)

½ teaspoon freshly ground black pepper

¼ cup (60 ml) cilantro, chopped

Curry Sauce:

1 tablespoon coconut oil

1 medium red onion, chopped

1½ teaspoons turmeric

½ teaspoon fennel seeds

½ teaspoon cumin seeds

2 teaspoons curry powder

1 (28-ounce) can (795 gr) organic diced tomatoes

½ cup (120 ml) chicken stock (see p. 206)

1 teaspoon ground cumin

½ teaspoon tikka masala

⅛ teaspoon nutmeg

⅛ teaspoon ground cinnamon

½ cup (120 ml) heavy cream

Sea salt

Rice and Toppings:

1 recipe brown rice (see p. 207)

½ cup (70 gr) cashews

¼ cup (60 ml) toasted coconut

¼ cup (60 ml) chopped cilantro

Place chicken, yogurt, tikka masala, black pepper, and cilantro in a large mixing bowl. Pierce each piece of chicken with a fork a few times. Cover bowl and marinate overnight in the refrigerator for at least 1 hour at room temperature.

Heat coconut oil over medium-high heat in a large skillet. When oil melts, add onion and sauté until soft and just beginning to caramelize, about 5 minutes. Make a well in the center of the onions and add the turmeric, fennel seeds, cumin seeds, and curry powder. Stir, keeping the spices in the center of the pan, for about 45 seconds, until you can smell the strong aroma of the spices. Stir spices into the onions and add the tomatoes. Lower the heat to medium and let the spiced tomatoes simmer for about 8–10 minutes, until thickened slightly.

Take the skillet off the heat. Using a hand immersion blender, puree the tomatoes into a chunky soup. (You can also do this in batches in the blender.) Drain marinated chicken and add to the tomatoes.

Put skillet back on the stove and cook chicken and tomatoes for 8–10 minutes over medium heat until cooked through. Stir in chicken stock and simmer again for another 10 minutes. While simmering, heat cumin in small sauté pan over medium heat until fragrant, about 1 minute. Add the tikka masala, nutmeg, cinnamon, and toasted cumin to the chicken and tomatoes. Pour in the heavy cream. Simmer for about 5 minutes. Season with salt to taste. Serve with hot bowls of brown rice and top with cashews, toasted coconut, and cilantro.

How Sweet It Is!

Sweet Tooth Tips

- When buying chocolate, look for one that is free of soy lecithin or one that uses non-GM (non-genetically modified) soy lecithin. (Numerous studies point to chocolate's significant heart benefits, especially dark chocolate.)

- An important switch to make is buying organic berries because conventional berries often are highly tainted with pesticides.

- Since we can overdo wholesome sweeteners, always use them in moderation.

- Instead of sodas that are full of high fructose corn syrup, try kombucha. It's a fizzy, sweet drink made from the kombucha mushroom and full of probiotics that help build healthy bacteria in your digestive system.

- Drink your tea with a sprinkle of Stevia—a natural sweetener that gives you lots of sweetness minus the chemicals.

- Read the labels and avoid man-made sweeteners such as corn syrup, sugar, sucrose, fructose, dextrose, and all artificial sweeteners. Instead, use natural sweeteners such as maple syrup, whole cane sugar, raw honey, Stevia and others.

CHAPTER EIGHT

Desserts

My Sweet Trio: Hannah, Pete and Abby

Desserts

Chocolate Chip Cookies

My mom is well known in Dallas for her gourmet chocolate-chip cookie dough. Converting her recipe into one that uses whole wheat flour and other organic ingredients was no easy feat. I was determined not to sacrifice taste for healthier ingredients. As a result, I prefer to use organic chocolate chips that do not contain lecithin or other additives (I usually buy them online) because when baked the chips are ultra-creamy. This is the recipe I'm most proud of in this book. Enjoy!

MAKES 2 DOZEN COOKIES

1 cup (110 gr) rolled oats, ground fine in a food processor or blender

2 cups (130 gr) whole wheat pastry flour, preferably freshly ground

1 ½ cups (225 gr) whole wheat flour, preferably freshly ground

1 ¼ teaspoons salt

1 ½ teaspoons baking soda

1 cup (230 gr) butter, softened

1 cup (185 gr) whole cane sugar or Sucanat (see p. 18)

1 cup (120 gr) muscovado sugar (see tip below)

2 teaspoons vanilla extract (see p. 212)

2 large eggs

2 cups (190 gr) semisweet chocolate chips

Preheat oven to 350°F (180°C) and adjust rack to middle position. Line two cookie sheets with parchment paper, as shown to the right.

Stir together oats, whole wheat pastry flour, whole wheat flour, salt, and baking soda in a medium bowl. Beat butter in a large bowl with electric or standing mixer on medium speed until creamy, about 1 minute. Add cane and muscovado sugars and beat until combined. Add vanilla and then eggs, one at a time. Scrape sides of bowl. With mixer on low, gradually add the dry ingredients until just combined. Stir in chocolate chips.

Scoop cookie dough onto lined baking sheets using a 2-inch (5.1 cm) cookie scoop. Bake for 12–14 minutes, until set and golden brown on top.

Be sure to check the Live Addendum on the IFP website for a list of my favorite sources for the chocolate chips and other ingredients in this book. Muscovado sugar, which is a dark brown sugar that is essential to the moist texture of these cookies, can be found at most specialty grocery stores or online. For more about different types of whole wheat flours for baking. see p. 23.

Strawberries and Cream Tart

This eye-catching tart is simply elegant and tastes divine. **SERVES 8**

::

Tart Crust:

1 ½ cups (195 gr) whole wheat pastry flour

¼ cup (45 gr) whole cane sugar or Sucanat (see p. 18)

½ cup (115 gr) unsalted butter, chilled and cut into

1-inch (2.5 cm) pieces

3 ounces (85 gr) bittersweet chocolate, chopped fine

20-24 strawberries, hulled

2 ounces (55 gr) bittersweet chocolate, melted and cooled

Pastry Cream:

¼ cup (60 ml) maple syrup

1 tablespoon arrowroot

1 large egg yolk

1 large egg

¾ cup (180 ml) whole milk

1 tablespoon unsalted butter

¼ teaspoon almond extract

::

Preheat oven to 350°F (180°C) and adjust rack to middle position. Using a pastry brush, grease a 9-inch (23 cm) removable-bottom tart pan with a little butter or coconut oil.

Pulse flour and whole cane sugar in a food processor until mixed. Add butter and pulse 15–17 times until dough begins to come together. Add a tablespoon of room temperature water and pulse 2–3 more times until dough is moist, but not tacky. If dough is still dry, add one more tablespoon of water. Pour dough out onto a piece of plastic wrap on the counter and press into a ball. Wrap plastic around dough and then flatten into a disk. Freeze dough for 10 minutes or refrigerate for 30 minutes.

Roll dough onto lightly floured surface to ⅛-inch (3 mm) thick round and transfer to tart pan, pressing dough in bottom and up sides of pan. Freeze for 10 minutes. Line the crust with parchment paper and then fill with pie weights or beans (I use ramekins). Bake crust for 15 minutes. Remove weights and parchment paper and bake until crisp and golden, about 15 minutes. Sprinkle chopped chocolate evenly over warm crust. Let sit for 5 minutes. Spread the now-melted chocolate evenly over crust. Cool completely.

Whisk together maple syrup, arrowroot, egg yolk, and egg in a mixing bowl. Heat milk over medium heat in a medium saucepan until steaming. Slowly pour milk into egg custard, whisking constantly, and then pour back into empty saucepan. Cook over medium heat, whisking until filling thickens and comes to a low boil. Remove from heat. Add butter and almond extract. Stir until butter melts. Pour pastry cream into a bowl and press parchment paper over surface (to keep a skin from forming on cream). Refrigerate 30–40 minutes or until cool.

Spread pastry cream evenly over chocolate-covered crust. Place berries on tart in a pattern of your choice (I love to place them upside down). Drizzle melted chocolate over strawberries. Serve immediately.

Chocolate Cream Pie

This silky, smooth, deep chocolate pie is my husband's favorite. Need I say more?

SERVES 8

::

Cookie Crust:

10 large chocolate chip cookies, about 2 cups (480 gr), crushed in food processor (see p. 168)

2 tablespoons unsalted butter, melted

Chocolate Cream Filling:

7 ounces (200 gr) mascarpone cheese, room temperature

2 large egg yolks

1 teaspoon vanilla extract (see p. 212)

½ cup (120 ml) whole milk

2 tablespoons maple syrup

1 cup (240 ml) chocolate sauce (see p. 208)

Topping:

2 cups (480 ml) heavy cream

1 teaspoon vanilla extract (see p. 212)

3 tablespoons maple syrup

::

Preheat oven to 350°F (180°C) and adjust oven rack to middle position.

Pour cookie crumbs and melted butter in a food processor and process until all the crumbs are uniformly fine and moist. Press crumbs into the sides and bottom of a 9-inch (23 cm) Pyrex pie plate. Bake the crust for 12 minutes. Remove from oven and lower oven heat to 325°F (160°C).

Whisk together the mascarpone cheese, egg yolks and vanilla in a small bowl. Whisk in the milk, maple syrup, and chocolate sauce. Pour filling onto warm crust and bake for 20–25 minutes, until edges are set. The middle will still jiggle, but will harden when cooled. Let the pie cool for about 10 minutes. Cover with parchment paper and let the paper touch the filling so it won't form a skin while cooling. Cool pie to room temperature and then re-frigerate for 4 hours.

Just before serving, pour heavy cream, vanilla, and maple syrup into mixing bowl attached to a standing mixer, or use an electric mixer. Whisk on high until soft peaks form, about 2 minutes. Remove parchment paper from cooled chocolate filling. Spread whipped cream on top of the pie and serve immediately.

Apple Blackberry Cobbler

When the air turns chilly, there are few things more comforting than ending your day with a bowl of warm cobbler topped with cream. Apples and blackberries are my favorite combination, but feel free to substitute other berries. **SERVES 8**

Filling:

3 apples, preferably Gala, peeled and cut into large bite-size pieces

2 cups (250 gr) blackberries, fresh or frozen

Zest of 1 lemon

Zest of 1 orange

2 tablespoons lemon juice

2 tablespoons orange juice

2 tablespoons whole wheat pastry flour

⅓ cup (60 gr) whole cane sugar or Sucanat (see p. 18)

½ teaspoon ground cinnamon

Topping:

1 cup (130 gr) whole wheat pastry flour

¾ cup (140 gr) whole cane sugar or Sucanat (see p. 18)

2 tablespoons maple syrup

¼ teaspoon sea salt

½ cup (115 gr) unsalted butter, cut into 8 pieces

½ cup (55 gr) rolled oats

½ cup (120 ml) heavy cream, optional

Preheat oven to 350°F (180°C) and adjust oven rack to middle position.

Mix apples, blackberries, lemon and orange zests, lemon, and orange juices, flour, cane sugar, and cinnamon in a large bowl. Pour fruit into a large 2-quart (1.9 liter) buttered baking dish.

Pulse together flour, cane sugar, maple syrup, and salt in a food processor—about 4 (1-second) pulses. Add the butter and pulse 10 (1-second pulses) until butter is incorporated. Add oats and pulse again 3–4 times to thoroughly combine. Topping should have large crumbles. Divide evenly over the fruit.

Bake for 45–50 minutes until top is golden brown and fruit is bubbly. Serve warm with a drizzle of cream on top, if you so desire.

VARIATION: See **Soaked Method** (p. 23). Soak the oats in ½ cup (120 ml) water and 1 tablespoon lemon juice at room temperature overnight. The next day, preheat the oven to 150°F (65°C). Spread oats in a single layer on a sheet pan and bake until crispy, 6–8 hours. Use these oats in the topping instead of the rolled oats. Substitute sprouted flour for the whole wheat pastry flour and follow directions above.

Panna Cotta

This is a popular "girly" dessert because it's smooth, creamy, and not too sweet. Top with seasonal berries, and you have the perfect light dessert. **SERVES 6**

:::

1 cup (240 ml) whole milk

2 ¾ teaspoons unflavored gelatin

3 cups (700 ml) heavy cream

⅓ cup (80 ml) honey

2 teaspoons vanilla extract (see p. 212)

1 cup (about 150 gr) seasonal berries

:::

Pour milk into a medium saucepan and sprinkle evenly with the gelatin. Let the milk sit for 5–10 minutes to allow the gelatin to soften.

Heat the milk and gelatin over medium heat, stirring constantly, until gelatin is dissolved and milk begins to steam. Stir the cream and honey into the warm milk and whisk until all the ingredients are dissolved. Remove the pan from the heat and stir in the vanilla. Let the cream cool for about 10 minutes.

Divide cream evenly among 6 glasses or small bowls. Cover panna cottas tightly with plastic wrap, making sure the plastic wrap does not touch the cream's surface. Refrigerate for about 5 hours, until cold and set. When you are ready to serve, top with seasonal berries.

Toffee Apple Pie

I have been making this pie since I first got married. I used to buy toffee at the store, but then realized that whole cane sugar, and butter simmered together makes a superb toffee without any artificial ingredients. The homemade toffee and apples meld together to produce a sugary caramel filling, surrounded by a flaky, buttery crust. It's simply hard to resist. **SERVES 8**

Toffee:

1 cup (185 gr) whole cane sugar or Sucanat (see p. 18)

1 cup (230 gr) unsalted butter

Apple Filling:

5 Granny Smith apples, cored, peeled and thinly sliced

1 tablespoon unsalted butter, melted and cooled

½ cup (95 gr) whole cane sugar or Sucanat (see p. 18)

2 tablespoons arrowroot

1 teaspoon cinnamon

Topping:

3 tablespoons unsalted butter, cold

¼ cup (45 gr) whole cane sugar or Sucanat (see p. 18)

½ teaspoon ground cinnamon

½ cup (65 gr) whole wheat pastry flour, freshly ground preferred

¼ cup (25 gr) pecans

1 unbaked baked pie crust (see p. 202)

Whisk together whole cane sugar, butter, and 3 tablespoons water in a medium saucepan and place over medium-high heat. Bring to a boil, and whisk constantly until liquid reaches 300°F (150°C), about 15 minutes. Remove from heat and immediately pour toffee onto a baking sheet lined with parchment paper. Spread evenly so toffee is about ½-inch (13 mm) thick. Cool completely. Chop into bite-size pieces.

Preheat oven to 350°F (180°C) and adjust oven rack to middle position.

Stir together apples, melted butter, cane sugar, arrowroot, cinnamon, and ¼ cup (60 ml) toffee pieces in a large bowl. Pour apples into pie crust.

Pulse together butter, whole cane sugar, cinnamon, and flour in food processor until crumbly. Add ¼ cup (60 ml) toffee pieces and pecans. Pulse 4–5 times until pecans and toffee are incorporated. Spread topping evenly over apples.

Bake apple pie for 45–55 minutes until apples are tender and crust is deep golden brown.

Raspberry Velvet Tart

White chocolate and raspberries make a beautiful and decadent combination for a tart. Be sure to bake the crust until it's crisp and golden. **SERVES 6**

Tart Crust:

1 ½ cups (195 gr) whole wheat pastry flour

¼ cup (45 gr) whole cane sugar or Sucanat (see p. 18)

½ cup (115 gr) unsalted butter, chilled and cut into 1-inch (2.5 cm) pieces

Filling:

12 ounces (340 gr) white chocolate, chopped

½ cup (120 ml) heavy cream, warmed

¼ cup (60 gr) unsalted butter, room temperature

3 cups (375 gr) fresh raspberries

Pulse flour and cane sugar in a food processor until mixed. Add butter and pulse 15–17 times until dough begins to come together. Add a tablespoon of water and pulse 2–3 more times until dough is moist, but not tacky. If dough is still dry, add 1–2 more tablespoons of water. Pour dough out onto a piece of plastic wrap on the counter and press into a ball. Wrap plastic around dough and then flatten into a disk. Freeze dough for 10 minutes or refrigerate for 30 minutes.

Preheat oven to 350°F (180°C) and adjust rack to middle position.

Roll dough onto lightly floured surface to ⅛-inch (3 mm) thick round and transfer to tart pan, pressing dough in bottom and up sides of pan. (Or use a rectangular tart pan and roll your dough into ⅛-inch (3 mm) thick rectangle to fit pan.) Freeze for 10 minutes. Line the crust with parchment paper and then fill with pie weights or beans (I use ramekins). Bake crust for 15 minutes. Remove weights and parchment paper and bake until crisp and golden, about 15 minutes. Cool completely.

Melt white chocolate in a large, heat-proof bowl set over a pot of simmering water. When chocolate is melted, slowly whisk in cream and butter. Stir until smooth. Spread raspberries evenly over crust and pour white chocolate cream over them.

Refrigerate, uncovered, for 2 hours before serving.

Bananas Foster

Bananas Foster is a classic Southern dessert that is enchanting to serve. Flaming the liquor at the end always provides a "wow" factor. This is my organic version of this crowd-pleaser. **SERVES 4**

¼ cup (55 gr) unsalted butter

¾ cup (140 gr) whole cane sugar or Sucanat (see p. 18)

½ teaspoon ground cinnamon

4 bananas, peeled and cut in half lengthwise

¼ cup (60 ml) good rum (I prefer Papagayo organic rum)

Vanilla ice cream

Combine the butter, cane sugar, cinnamon, and 2 tablespoons water over low heat in a large skillet. Stir constantly until the sugar dissolves and creates a thick sauce.

Place bananas in the pan and sauté on each side for about 2 minutes until golden brown. Add the rum, tip the pan to the side, and ignite the rum with a lit match or lighter. When the flames subside, immediately serve over vanilla ice cream.

Cherry Rhubarb Crisp

I can never seem to remember the difference between a crumble, crisp, Betty, or cobbler. I call this recipe a crisp because I feel it's the most fitting. I love the sourness of fresh rhubarb paired with the burst of sweetness from cherries. I prefer to use fresh fruit, but frozen will work just as well. The topping of oats, butter, and whole cane sugar couldn't be a better picture of summer for me. **SERVES 6-8**

Oatmeal Crust:

1 cup (100 gr) pecans

1 ½ cups (165 gr) rolled oats

1 cup (130 gr) whole wheat pastry flour, preferably freshly ground

1 cup (185 gr) whole cane sugar or Sucanat (see p. 18)

½ cup (115 gr) plus 2 tablespoons unsalted butter, cold, cut into small pieces

½ cup (120 ml) whipped cream or fresh raw cream

Filling:

1 cup (185 gr) whole cane sugar or Sucanat (see p. 18)

3 tablespoons arrowroot

2 teaspoons almond extract

10 ounces (285 gr) fresh or frozen cherries, pitted

4 cups (450 gr) rhubarb, fresh or frozen, cut into 1-inch (2.5 cm) pieces

Preheat oven to 350°F (180°C) and adjust rack to middle position. Butter an 11 x 7-inch (28 x 18 cm) baking dish.

Process the pecans, oats, flour, and cane sugar in a food processor until blended, about four 1-second pulses. Add the butter and pulse until crumbs begins to gather. Add a few tablespoons of water if the topping appears too crumbly.

Whisk together cane sugar, arrowroot, and ½ cup (120 ml) water in a medium saucepan over medium heat. Whisk constantly until simmering. When the liquid comes to a boil, let it remain at a boil for 1 minute while continuing to whisk. Remove from heat and stir in the almond extract.

Press half of oatmeal crust in the bottom of the baking dish. Pour the rhubarb and cherries on top and spread out to distribute evenly. Pour the sugar mixture over the fruit and top with the remaining oatmeal crust.

Bake for 40–45 minutes. Serve warm with a dollop of whipped cream, or drizzle with fresh raw cream on top.

Strawberry Chocolate Cream Cheese Cupcakes

The deep chocolate cake, strawberry filling, cream cheese frosting, and melted chocolate topping create a combination that's like a party in your mouth.

MAKES 12 CUPCAKES

::

Chocolate Cupcakes:

½ cup (120 ml) unsalted butter

¼ cup (60 ml) chocolate sauce (see p. 208)

½ cup (40 gr) cacao powder

1 cup (130 gr) whole wheat pastry flour

½ teaspoon baking soda

¾ teaspoon baking powder

2 large eggs

¾ cup (140 gr) whole cane sugar or Sucanat (see p. 18)

1 teaspoon vanilla extract (see p. 212)

½ teaspoon sea salt

½ cup (120 ml) sour cream

½ cup (120 ml) strawberry preserves

Strawberry Cream Cheese Frosting:

8 ounces (230 gr) cream cheese, room temperature

5 tablespoons unsalted butter, room temperature

1 tablespoon sour cream

5 tablespoons strawberry preserves

½ cup (120 ml) chocolate sauce (see p. 208)

::

Heat oven to 350°F (180°C) and adjust oven rack to middle position. Line a muffin pan with unbleached muffin pan liners.

Melt butter in a double boiler over medium heat. Whisk in ¼ cup chocolate sauce and cacao.

Sift flour over a large bowl. Up to about ¼ cup (30 gr) of the outside layer of the wheat may be left over; throw out and use only the remaining ¾ cup (100 gr) flour. Whisk in the baking soda and baking powder.

In another large mixing bowl, whisk together eggs, whole cane sugar, vanilla, and salt. Add chocolate mixture and whisk to combine. Add ⅓ of dry ingredients and whisk until combined. Whisk in sour cream and then add the rest of the dry ingredients. Continue to whisk until batter is uniform and thick.

Divide batter evenly into a muffin pan and bake for 20–22 minutes or until a skewer inserted in a cupcake comes out clean. Cool cupcakes to room temperature.

Spoon strawberry preserves into a piping bag with a large round tip attached at the end.

Push the tip into the top of each cupcake and squeeze about a tablespoon of preserves into the middle. If the tip gets clogged with cake, simply squeeze the pastry bag to release the cake.

Whisk together cream cheese, butter, sour cream, and strawberry preserves in a large bowl until well combined. Frost each cupcake. Spoon remaining ½ cup chocolate sauce over frosting.

VARIATION: See **Soaked Method** (p. 23). Sift flour over a large bowl. About ¼ cup (30 gr) of the outside layer of the wheat will be left over; throw out and use the remaining ¾ cup (100 gr) flour. Stir together flour and sour cream. Cover tightly and leave at room temperature overnight. The next day, line a muffin pan with unbleached muffin liners. Melt butter over low heat in a medium saucepan. Whisk in ¼ cup chocolate sauce and cacao. Stir together the soaked flour, baking soda and baking powder. Whisk together eggs, cane sugar, vanilla, and salt in a mixing bowl of a standing mixer or by using an electric mixer. Add chocolate mixture and whisk to combine. Turn mixer on low and slowly add the soaked flour, one large spoonful at a time. Mix until the batter is uniform and thick. Proceed with recipe above where it says, "Divide batter evenly."

Chocolate Mousse

Rich and thick, this light and easy-to-make chocolate mousse is sparked by a touch of herbal coffee. **SERVES 6**

½ cup (115 gr) unsalted butter

½ cup (120 ml) plus 1 tablespoon maple syrup

½ cup (65 gr) plus 2 tablespoons cacao powder

1 teaspoon vanilla extract (see p. 212)

Pinch of sea salt

1 teaspoon instant herbal coffee

3 large egg yolks

3 teaspoons maple syrup

⅛ teaspoon sea salt

3 large egg whites

1 cup (240 ml) heavy cream

Combine butter, ½ cup (120 ml) plus 1 tablespoon maple syrup, cacao powder, vanilla, pinch of salt, herbal coffee, and 5 tablespoons water in a medium heat-proof bowl. Set bowl over saucepan filled with 1 inch (2.5 cm) of simmering water. Whisk frequently until smooth and remove from heat.

Whisk egg yolks, 1 ½ teaspoons maple syrup, and ⅛ teaspoon salt in a medium bowl, about 30 seconds, until it lightens in color. Add chocolate sauce and whisk until combined. Let cool until just above room temperature.

In a bowl of a standing mixer or with an electric mixer, whisk egg whites on low until frothy. Add remaining 1 ½ teaspoons maple syrup. Increase the speed to medium high and whisk until soft peaks form. Stir about ¼ of the egg whites into the chocolate liquid, and then fold in the remaining whites by scooping the egg whites into the mixture gently, cutting down the bowl, across, and up the other side. Rotate the bowl a quarter turn and keep folding until liquid and egg whites are combined.

Whip heavy cream until soft peaks form. Gently fold all of whipped cream into the chocolate liquid until no white streaks remain, using the folding technique above.

Ladle mousse into individual bowls. Cover and refrigerate until set and firm, about 2 hours.

If you don't have instant herbal coffee, use 2 tablespoons of brewed herbal coffee (such as Teeccino) and reduce the amount of water used in the recipe to 3 tablespoons.

Creamy Lemon Ice Cream

Creamy lemon ice cream is a treat that makes me think of hot summer days in Texas. It was a family tradition every Fourth of July to pull out our ice cream maker and churn lemon ice cream. Like all kids, my brothers and I would eagerly wait with spoons in hand for that first bite. **MAKES 1 QUART** (950 ML)

:::

½ cup (120 ml) honey
1 ½ tablespoons arrowroot
¾ cup (180 ml) heavy cream
Pinch of sea salt
2 cups (475 ml) sour cream or crème fraîche (see p. 200)
¼ cup (60 ml) plus 1 tablespoon fresh lemon juice

:::

Whisk honey, arrowroot, cream, and salt together in a medium saucepan over medium heat. Bring mixture to a simmer while whisking constantly for 1–2 minutes until it thickens.

Remove from heat and add the sour cream a little at a time, whisking quickly so it doesn't curdle. Whisk in the lemon juice and pour into a large bowl. Cover bowl tightly and refrigerate for about 3 hours, or until thoroughly chilled.

To speed up the process, fill a large bowl with ice and set the bowl of lemon cream on top. The cream should be cold enough to put into your ice cream maker in about 45 minutes. Freeze in your ice cream maker according to the manufacturer's instructions.

Coconut Cinnamon Ice Cream

Many ice creams sold at the grocery store have so many chemical additives and preservatives that the natural flavor of simple ingredients like cream or sugar is lost. Making your own ice cream allows you to know exactly what is going into your dessert. I make this ice cream with coconut milk for a dairy-free option, but you can easily substitute whole milk in its place. **MAKES 1 QUART** (950 ML)

3 cups (700 ml) coconut milk

¾ cup (180 ml) maple syrup

1 teaspoon ground cinnamon

2 large egg yolks

1 tablespoon vanilla extract (see p. 212)

1 cup (110 gr) dehydrated almonds, blanched and chopped (see p. 213)

1 recipe chocolate sauce, cold (see p. 208)

Blend coconut milk, maple syrup, cinnamon, egg yolks, and vanilla in a blender until smooth. Pour custard into ice cream maker and churn until thick and creamy.

Just before the ice cream is done, add the almonds and cold chocolate sauce slowly, 1 tablespoon at a time. When the almonds and chocolate are distributed throughout the ice cream, turn off the ice cream maker.

Give the ice cream a few good stirs with a large spoon to make sure the sauce and nuts are mixed into the ice cream evenly. Pour into a bowl, cover, and store in the freezer until ready to serve.

Maple Marshmallows

Every marshmallow recipe I found in the past used corn syrup, so I decided to create a healthier marshmallow using maple syrup instead. I discovered that if maple syrup is simmered to 240°F (115°C), it reacts a lot like corn syrup. This recipe is fun to make with kids because they're fascinated watching maple syrup, gelatin, and water turn into fluffy goodness. **MAKES 30 (2-INCH/5 CM) MARSHMALLOWS**

3 tablespoons unflavored gelatin
2 cups (475 ml) maple syrup
¼ teaspoon sea salt
1 tablespoon vanilla extract (see p. 212)

Sprinkle gelatin over ½ cup (120 ml) water in a bowl of a standing mixer with whisk attached. Set aside for 5 minutes so the gelatin can soften and bloom. Lightly oil a 13 x 9-inch (33 x 23 cm) baking dish.

Whisk together maple syrup and salt in a medium saucepan over medium heat. Gently simmer until syrup reaches 240°F (115°C). With mixer on medium speed, very slowly add maple syrup to gelatin and water in mixing bowl. Add vanilla and turn mixer on high for 10 minutes until liquid has doubled and becomes light and fluffy. Pour into dish and let sit overnight, uncovered.

The next day, flip the marshmallows onto a greased cutting board. Cut marshmallows using a knife dipped in hot water, to prevent sticking. Or use cookie cutters you have dipped in a little oil.

Simply Good

Tips on the Basics

- Find a good source for unrefined coconut oil. It should have a mild coconut aroma but not smell or taste sweet.

- Make a batch of dehydrated nuts (p. 213), put them in small containers to stash in your bag, purse, or car for a quick snack.

- Be adventurous. Incorporate a variety of whole grains in your diet that include quinoa, wild rice, and millet. Try new grains and find which ones are your favorites.

- Make chicken stock (p. 206) once a week and freeze it in ice cube trays so you can simply pull out the amount needed (and make chicken soup when the first sign of a cold appears).

- Replace processed vegetable oils with healthy nourishing fats such as butter, coconut oil, and olive oil.

- Store flax seed and hemp seeds in the freezer so they are available to add to smoothies or to sprinkle over your yogurt.

- Go to a specialty store and look for good vinegar. Use quality vinegars to splash on your salads and vegetables for added flavor.

- If you aren't ready to try raw milk, then purchase milk that is pasteurized, not ultra-pasteurized. They both have a 10-day shelf life.

CHAPTER NINE

The Basics

The Basics

Fresh Whole Wheat Linguine

If you've never made homemade pasta, this is a simple recipe to get you started. Flour and eggs are kneaded together and then rolled out to create a smooth and rich, eggy pasta. This will rival any dried pasta you can purchase at the store. The active prep time is about 25 minutes, and the dough stores in the refrigerator for two to three days. **MAKES 1 POUND OF FRESH PASTA**

2 ½ cups (350 gr) durum wheat flour
4 large eggs

Place durum wheat flour on the counter and make a well in the center. Crack eggs into the well and begin kneading the dough with your hands. Knead for 1–2 minutes until the dough becomes smooth and uniform, adding more flour as necessary. Cover the dough and let it rest for at least 15 minutes and up to 2 hours.

Bring a large pot of salted water to a boil. Cut dough in half and follow the pasta machine manufacturer's instructions for rolling and cutting the dough to the desired shape and size. If you do not have a pasta maker, roll the dough out into very thin sheets, about 1/16-inch (2 mm) thick, and cut with a sharp knife. As you cut the pasta into linguine, dust your pasta with flour to prevent it from sticking.

If you want to make the dough ahead of time, wrap the dough tightly and store in the fridge for up to two days. Let the dough come to room temperature before forming it into pasta.

Crème Fraîche

Crème fraîche is similar to sour cream, but it's thicker and smoother; and a small dollop goes a long way. I like to use it over berries or on desserts where traditionally whipped cream is spooned on top. You can even use it instead of sour cream on baked potatoes. Crème fraîche can be quite costly at the store and hard to find. This recipe is a quick, simple, and economical way to make your own.

MAKES 1 CUP (240 ML)

1 cup (240 ml) heavy cream

2 tablespoons buttermilk (see p. 203)

Whisk together cream and buttermilk in a small jar. Cover and leave at room temperature overnight, or until thick and creamy. Stir and then store covered in the refrigerator.

Pie Crust

After a lot of experimentation, I'm thrilled to give you a basic pie crust recipe that is free of white refined flour. The crust uses a mixture of whole wheat pastry flour, rice flour, and tapioca flour. These flours can all be found at most grocery stores. Keep in mind that this crust makes enough for two 9-inch (23 cm) pie crusts. If you don't need two crusts, freeze one for later use. **MAKES TWO PIE CRUSTS**

1 ½ cups (195 gr) whole wheat pastry flour
1 cup (150 gr) plus 2 tablespoons brown rice flour
¼ cup (40 gr) plus 2 tablespoons tapioca flour
1 ½ teaspoons sea salt
1 cup (230 gr) plus 3 tablespoons cold butter, cut into tablespoons

Place pastry flour, brown rice flour, tapioca flour, and salt in a food processor. Pulse a few times to combine. Add butter and pulse until it looks like wet sand, about 8 (1-second) pulses. Add 10 tablespoons of ice water, 1 tablespoon at a time, and pulse after each addition. Pulse until dough gathers into larger clumps. The dough should not be crumbly. If it is, add a tablespoon or two of water. Divide dough into 2 portions and wrap plastic wrap around each piece, pressing firmly to form into a disk. Refrigerate for 30 minutes.

Roll out dough on a generously floured surface into a 12-inch (30 cm) disk. Carefully roll dough loosely around the rolling pin and then unroll in pie dish. Fold the overhanging dough under itself and then crimp with your fingers or press against the lip of the pie dish with a fork. Add filling and bake according to pie directions.

For a pre-baked pie crust: Preheat oven to 350°F (180°C). After you have shaped the dough in the pie plate, refrigerate for 15 minutes. Cover dough with parchment paper and fill with pie weights or dried beans. Bake for 15 minutes. Remove the weights and parchment paper. Pierce the bottom of the crust with a fork every few inches and bake for another 5–10 minutes, until golden brown.

Buttermilk

There really isn't any need to buy buttermilk at the store when you can so easily make it at home. I always have a jar of it in my fridge to use in all kinds of baked goods. **MAKES 1 CUP** (240 ML)

:::

1 cup (240 ml) whole milk

1 ½ tablespoons lemon juice

:::

Whisk together milk and lemon juice in a small bowl. Cover and leave at room temperature overnight. Store, covered, in the refrigerator for up to 2 weeks.

Mayonnaise

Quick and simple with amazing flavor. **MAKES 1 CUP (240 ML)**

1 large egg yolk
¼ teaspoon sea salt
2 teaspoons lemon juice
1 teaspoon white wine vinegar
¼ teaspoon Dijon mustard
¾ cup (180 ml) light olive oil

Combine egg yolk, salt, lemon juice, vinegar, and mustard. Whisk together for about 30 seconds. Very slowly add the olive oil and whisk constantly until the liquid becomes thick. The mayonnaise keeps in the refrigerator for 1 week.

Chicken Stock

There's no comparison between homemade chicken stock and stock poured out of a can. The flavors are much deeper, and the quality of nutrients is far greater than anything you'll find wrapped in aluminum. Don't be intimidated by "making your own stock." It's quite simple—put all the ingredients in a pot and leave to simmer. That's it! **MAKES APPROXIMATELY 8 CUPS (1.9 LITERS)**

:::

1 (3–4 pound) chicken (1.4–1.8 kg), preferably pastured

2 carrots

1 stalk celery

1 large bunch parsley

1 head of garlic, cut in half

1 large onion, cut into quarters (don't worry about peeling it)

2 tablespoons sea salt

1 teaspoon vinegar

:::

Place all ingredients in large stockpot. Add just enough water to cover. Bring to a boil, skim foam off the top, and then let simmer for 6 hours, with lid ajar.

Strain broth. After the broth is cool it should gelatinize, but don't be alarmed. This is a sign that the nutrients were pulled out of the chicken.

 If you aren't going to use all the broth in the next few days, either freeze it in ice cube trays (so you can use a little at a time) or in a large bowl. The cubes will keep in a sealed container in the freezer for about two months.

Brown Rice

After I learned how to make brown rice using this method, I never went back. Each grain of brown rice opens, making it light and fluffy. I usually put the rice on the stove late in the day and leave it simmering until dinner. **SERVES 6-8**

2 tablespoons butter
2 tablespoons olive oil
2 cups (475 ml) organic long-grain brown rice
1 ½ tablespoons sea salt

Melt butter and olive oil in a large pot over medium heat. Add the rice and sauté for about 5 minutes, until the grains turns milky white. Add 4 cups (950 ml) water and sea salt. Boil for 8 minutes, uncovered. Reduce heat to the lowest setting, cover, and leave to cook 1 ½–2 hours until rice is cooked through.

Chocolate Sauce

This is the perfect chocolate sauce to drizzle over ice cream. It also makes a wonderful foundation to many chocolate dessert recipes. It is a handy thing to have in the fridge when the craving for chocolate arises. **MAKES ABOUT 1 CUP (240 ML)**

½ cup (115 gr) unsalted butter
½ cup (40 gr) cacao powder
¼ cup (60 ml) maple syrup
1 teaspoon vanilla extract (see p. 212)

Melt butter over medium heat in a small saucepan. Remove from heat and cool 5 minutes or until cool to touch. Whisk in cacao powder, maple syrup, and vanilla until blended. This sauce will keep in the refrigerator for 2 weeks.

 This sauce can be substituted in just about any recipe that calls for melted chocolate.

Movie Theater Popcorn

You may wonder why I'm including a recipe for popcorn. It's because my friends regularly ask how to make popcorn without a microwave. A friend gave me the tip of using red palm oil, which deepens the flavor and gives the popcorn the yellow color just like at the movies. I made it for my kids and their friends one afternoon, and one of the little girls said, "Mrs. Vitt, this is the most amazing popcorn I've ever had!" I hope you agree. **SERVES 6**

3 tablespoons coconut oil

3 tablespoons unsalted butter

2 teaspoons red palm oil

1 ½ cups (315 gr) popcorn

1 teaspoon sea salt

In a large Dutch oven melt the coconut oil, butter, and palm oil over medium-high heat. Add the popcorn and sea salt. Cover and shake to distribute the kernels and salt. Keep the lid on, and every 10 seconds or so, shake the pan to avoid burning. When popping declines dramatically, take pot off of heat and immediately pour into a large bowl.

Homemade Vanilla Extract

It's far more economical to make your own organic vanilla at home than buying it at the store. This recipe will last in your pantry for years, and you will always have preserved vanilla beans to use in your baking. **MAKES 12 OUNCES (350 ML)**

::

10 vanilla beans, whole or chopped
1 (24-ounce) Mason jar (700 ml), or other jar of your choice
1 ½ cups (375 ml) organic vodka

::

Place vanilla beans in the jar and pour vodka over the beans. Make sure the lid is on tight and store in a dark, cool place. If using whole beans, let the vanilla sit for 2 months. If you chopped your vanilla beans, let vanilla sit about 3 weeks before using. Shake bottle before each use. As you use up the vanilla, you can add more vodka to make the beans go further.

Dehydrated Nuts

These nuts are the perfect snack for road trips or soccer games. You can even keep them in a small bag in your purse as a handy snack for yourself or kids. This recipe was adapted from Sally Fallon's *Nourishing Traditions*. **MAKES 4 CUPS (950 ML)**

::

4 cups (400 gr) nuts (pecans, almonds, cashews, etc.)
1 tablespoon sea salt

::

Pour nuts in a large bowl and cover with water. Add salt and stir. Leave on counter overnight. The next day, preheat the oven to 150°F (65°C), drain the nuts, and spread out in a single layer on a baking sheet. Place the tray in the oven. Leave in the oven until dry and crispy. (I usually do this overnight.)

CHAPTER TEN

Menus

Menus

SOUTHWESTERN DINNER PARTY

BRUNCH

GAME DAY

PICNIC IN THE PARK

FARMER'S MARKET DINNER

ELEGANT DINNER

CHAPTER ELEVEN

Resources

Resources

You can obtain many of the ingredients in this book at your local health food store, but if you're in a small town, you may need other resources from time to time. Listed here are some of my favorites to get you started. Be sure to check out the regularly updated "Vendor Source List" on the Live Addendum for this book on IFP's website: www.ifpinc.com. When buying direct from suppliers, especially farms, review its safety record and make sure that it is in compliance with all local, state, and federal regulations—particularly when it comes to dairy and meat to ensure you are purchasing safe and wholesome food.

Online Sources

Sugars and Sweeteners

Organic Whole Cane Sugar
www.rapunzel.com

Sucanat
www.breadbeckers.com

Fermented Organic Soy Sauce

Ohsawa Organic Kosher Nama Shoyu
www.goldminenaturalfood.com

Olive Oil

Bariani Olive Oil
www.barianioliveoil.com

Coconut Oil (and other coconut products)

Wilderness Family Naturals
www.wildernessfamilynaturals.com

Tropical Traditions
www.tropicaltraditions.com

Whole Grains

Organic hard and soft wheat are easily accessible now. At large grocery stores, like Whole Foods, you can even get your wheat ground fresh for you right there in the store. Here, however, is my favorite source for grains.

The Bread Beckers
www.breadbeckers.com

Sprouted Wheat Flour

This is wonderful flour, already sprouted, and best for baking breads. I like to keep a bag in the freezer for those occasions when I want to make a quick bread before a meal.

www.organicsproutedflour.net

Organic Raw Milk

www.organicpastures.com

www.realmilk.com

Organic Meats

www.eatwild.com

www.peacefulpastures.com

www.heritagefarms.com

www.grasslandbeef.com

Organic Chocolate

www.greenandblacks.com

www.dagobachocolate.com

Cacao Powder

www.wildernessfamilynaturals.com

www.rapunzel.com

Gelatin

www.bernardjensen.com

Organic Spices and Teas

www.mountainroseherbs.com

Organic (and affordable) Nuts

www.nutsonline.com

Organic Sulfite-Free Wine

www.freywine.com

Sea Salt

www.celticseasalt.com

Organic Liquor

www.maisonjomere.com

Organic Tequila

www.4copas.com

Herbal Coffee:

www.teeccino.com

www.dandyblend.com

Honey

www.reallyrawhoney.com

Hemp Seeds

www.nutiva.com

For other grocery items you cannot find locally:

www.azurestandard.com

Recommended Reading Web Sites

Deliciously Organic Blog

www.deliciouslyorganic.blogspot.com

Weston A. Price Foundation

www.westonaprice.org

Environmental Working Group

www.ewg.org

Take Part

www.takepart.com

The Center for Food Safety

www.truefoodnow.org

Dr. Mercola

www.mercola.com

Local Harvest

www.localharvest.org

Organic Coupons

www.mambosprouts.com

Recommended Reading

In Defense of Food
Michael Pollan (Penguin, 2009)

The Cholesterol Myths
Uffe Ravnskov, M.D., Ph.D. (NewTrends Publishing, Inc., 2002)

Eat Fat, Lose Fat
Dr. Mary Enig and Sally Fallon (Plume, 2006)

The Maker's Diet
Jordan Rubin (Siloam Press, 2005)

Nourishing Traditions
Sally Fallon (NewTrends Publishing, Inc., 1999)
I especially recommend reading about soaking grains in her book, starting on p. 25.

The Omnivores Dilemma
Michael Pollan (Penguin, 2007)

Dying to Look Good

Christine Hoza Farlow, DC (Kiss for Health Publishing, 2000)

The Untold Story of Milk: Revised and Updated

Ron Schmid, ND (NewTrends Publishing, Inc., 2007)

Further References

Internet article: "Don't drink your milk!"

www.mercola.com

Internet: Irradiation

www.centerforfoodsafety.org/food_irrad.cfm

Internet article: "Milk: It Does a Body Good?"

www.westonaprice.org

Index

er earthy fresh non-toxic leafy sweet

agrant living edible local herbal tasty

rt free-range colorful tender robust

natural juicy green ripe wholesome

nutritional accessible pure raw healthy

olesome tender earthy fresh non-toxic

isp robust fragrant living edible local

fibrous tart free-range colorful raw

local herbal tasty natural juicy green

toxic leafy sweet nutritional accessible

agrant living edible local herbal tasty

natural juicy green ripe wholesome t

nutritional colorful tender crisp robust

accessible pure raw healthy fibrous

fragrant living edible local herbal t

tender earthy fresh non-toxic leafy sw

fibrous tart natural juicy green ripe

leafy sweet nutritional colorful tender

herbal tasty accessible pure raw heal

tender crisp robust fragrant living edi

ripe wholesome tender earthy fresh n

pure raw healthy fibrous tart robust